Horary Astrology

Geraldine Davis

Copyright 2017 by American Federation of Astrologers, Inc.

No part of this book may be reproduced or transcribed in any form or by any means, electronic or mechanical, including photocopying or recording or by any information storage and retrieval system without written permission from the author and publisher, except in the case of brief quotations embodied in critical reviews and articles. Requests and inquiries may be mailed to: American Federation of Astrologers, Inc., 6535 S. Rural Road, Tempe, AZ 85283.

ISBN-13: 978-0-86690-667-8

Cover Design: Jack Cipolla

Published by:
American Federation of Astrologers, Inc.
6535 S. Rural Road
Tempe, AZ 85283

Dedication

I wish to dedicate this book to my students and colleagues of astrology and to my teacher and friend, Harriet K. Banes.

Contents

Preface	xi
Introduction	xiii

Chart Components

The Zodiac	1
The Ten Planets	2
The Asteroids	3
The Moon's Nodes	3
The Part of Fortune	3
The Aspects	4
The Effect of the Aspects	5
Terms used in Horary Astrology	6
The Measure of Time	10
The Directions by Houses	11
The Directions by Signs	11
The Twelve Departments of Life	11
Dignities and Debilities of Planets	13
Countries and Cities Ruled by the Zodiacal Signs	15
About Colors	17
The Kinds of Employment Ruled by Each Planet	20
Planets in Business	22
The Moon's Power	23
The Moon as Significator and Some Important Considerations	24 / 24
Personal Description of the Twelve Signs and Planets in the Signs and the Disposition Produced by the Signs	26
Questions Relating to Each of the Twelve Houses and the Meaning of the Planets in the Houses	57
Whether the Question is Radical or Fit to be Judged	75

v

Horary Questions by House

First House Questions	77
What Part of Life is Likely to be Fortunate?	77
Duration of the Physical Life	77
The Nature of the Death	79
Where Shall He Go to Better Himself?	79
Questions Concerning an Absent Person	80
Ship at Sea and its Voyage	81
Will the Voyage Prove Prosperous?	82
Will the Voyage be Long or Short?	83
Of Bills and Promissory Notes	84
Second House Questions	85
Whether the Querent Will Gain All He Expects	85
Instructions	86
Of Riches or Gain	87
Testimonies of Poverty	88
By What Means Will the Querent Obtain Riches?	88
Cause of Poverty or Hindrance of Gain	90
The Time When the Querent May Obtain Riches	91
Will the Querent Receive His Wages or Salary?	91
Third House Questions	91
Of Absent Brothers, Sisters, Cousins, Neighbors, Children or Friends, etc.	94
Questions Regarding Agreements Between Brethren and Neighbors	94
Is it Well to go on a Short Journey?	94
An Agreeable Journey	95
Of Anonymous Letters	96
Whether a Report is True or False	96
Fourth House Questions	97
Questions About Property in General	97
Will it be Best for Me to Buy Property?	98
Will I Buy the Property?	98
Buying and Selling in General	99
What is the Quality and Value of the Property?	99

Questions About Moving	102
The Time the Querent Will Move	102
Will the Querent Inherit the Property?	103
Of Treasures, Mines, etc. Whether Recoverable or Not	104
There Is No Treasure, Etc.	104
Of Besieged Places	105
Places and Things Ruled by the Signs and Planets	105
Of Things Mislaid or Hidden; Where to Find Them	108
Example Charts	109
Fifth House Questions in General, Lotteries, Prizes, Prize Money, Raffles, Games, Cards, Horse Races, Football, Amusements, Winning a Bet or Wager	119
Information Regarding Football Games, Etc.	120
Whether a Woman Will Have Children	123
To Find How Many Children a Woman Will Have	123
A Woman Asks if She Is With Child	124
Will the Child be a Boy or Girl?	125
Will There Be Twins?	128
Length of Time a Woman Has Been Pregnant	128
Time of Birth	128
Whether a Child Will Live or Die	129
About Lost or Runaway Children	129
Of a Messenger Sent on Important Business	130
What Takes Place on the Journey	131
The Time of the Messenger's Return Home	131
The Character of the Messenger	132
Sixth House Questions	132
Of Servants, Lodgers or Tenants in General	132
If the Question is About a Tenant's Removal	133
How to Attain Health and What Causes Sickness	134
How to Judge Questions Pertaining to Sickness and Disease in General	137
The Hyleg, Life and Death, and Medication	139
The Physical Health	142

Questions Concerning Small Animals, Such as Chickens, 151
Turkeys, Sheep, Pigs, Calves, Birds, Dogs, Cats
and Other Pets
Questions Concerning Lost, Strayed or Stolen Animals 152
Seventh House Questions 152
Questions About Love and Marriage 152
Will the Woman Marry? 153
Planets and Aspects That Hinder Marriage 154
The Time the Marriage Will Take Place 155
How the Parties Will Agree in Marriage 156
Which of the Two is Best Connected? 157
Will the Querent Marry More Than Once? 157
Whether the Man or Wife Will Die First 158
Has the Lady Another Affair? 158
Has the Gentleman Another Affair? 159
Will the Husband or Wife Return? 160
A Woman Leaving Her Husband 160
May I Enter Into Partnership or Society? 161
Shall We Succeed in Business Partnership? 162
Which Will Be Best Qualified? 162
Lawsuits 163
You May Prevent a Lawsuit and Be Reconciled 163
Who Will Win the Lawsuit? 164
How the Judge or Lawyer Will Decide the Case 164
Will the Bankruptcy Action Be Successful? 165
On the Recovery of Debts 166
Will It Be Safe to Cash a Check, etc. 167
Shall I Return Safe From War? 167
Answers to Questions About War 168
Whether Two Armies Will Fight 170
Has the Querent Public Enemies? 171
Of Theft Questions in General 171
To Find Out Who the Thief Is 172
Will the Stolen Articles Be Recovered 174
When to Sell Large Cattle 175

Eighth House Questions, Such as Premiums, Retirement 176
    Money, Social Security, Pensions, Wills
Legacies   172
Will the Querent Obtain the Expected Legacy?   178
Persons and Circumstances Obstructing Inheritance   178
    or Legacies
Will the Wife's or Husband's Portion Be Obtained?   179
Will I Live With My Parents?   181
Shall We Have Death in the Family Soon?   181
Ninth House Questions   181
Of Carrying Insurance or Indemnity Policies   181
Of the Success of Books, etc.   182
Of Profit Through Science and Higher Education   183
Will the Clergyman or Professor Obtain   183
    the Appointment?
Tenth House Questions   184
When Shall I Obtain a Situation?   184
Shall I Prosper in Business?   186
Shall I Obtain This Situation?   186
Shall I Continue in my Present Situation   187
Shall I Leave my Present Situation?   187
What Will Be the Cause of Leaving?   188
Of the Success of a Petition to Any Person in Power   188
Whether an Exile Will Be Restored   189
Eleventh House Questions, Including Group   190
    Legislation, Reforming of Matrimonial Laws,
    New Inventions, Adjustment of Relationships
Shall I Obtain My Hope, Wish, or Whatever   191
    Pertains to Eleventh House Affairs?
What Kind of a Person Will Prove to be My Best Friend? 192
Is This Person a Friend to Me?   193
Twelfth House Questions, Including: Circumstances   194
    Pertaining to Enforced Labor Conditions, Advanced
    Therapeutic Procedure Combining Medical and
    Metaphysical Methods

Questions About Private Enemies	195
How Much Power Do They Possess	196
There: Are No Private Enemies	196
Of Imprisonment or Banishment	197
Persons Transported or in Any Way Exiled	197
Elections	198
Election for a Journey	201

Preface

This text book on horary astrology is compiled and published for the benefit and use of all students interested in and studying this practical branch of the work. I wish to acknowledge the valuable assistance rendered by Josephine Leask for typing and assisting me in compiling my composition for this publication.

During my years of study and research, I have used the different text books on this subject, but my authority in teaching is Dr. W. J. Simonite, whose manual is now out of print.

The oft repeated wish and request of students interested in this work for practical rules has caused me to compile and publish this text book with the sincere wish that everyone may derive as much satisfaction and benefit from the use of these rules as I have. It will then serve the purpose for which it is written. It is not perfect, because I myself am not perfect.

This branch of astrology is fast becoming popular; there is certainly no other branch of the science more practical. We all have everyday problems that need solving in a workable, scientific way. If the tried and tested rules given in this book are used, any question may be answered with satisfaction and accuracy. However, all the rules in the world are useless without study and application. From research and application we gain experience and knowledge; this, in turn, gives us assurance.

We create our own power as we develop our own mentalities. Truth, courage, and the desire to serve cheerfully and selflessly, coupled with our trained mentality, will always stand the hardest tests. Intellectual ideas, if they are familiar, recur to us at will. Confidence is the mental attribute that all of us, who wish to serve, should seek to cultivate. If we doubt our own ability, how can we convince others?

Introduction

We have all the proof we need that astrology is the oldest science in existence, not only pre-historic but pre-traditional. It is the science of the effect of the solar and planetary currents on our earth, particularly as they affect the living things of our earth and the directions and indications of the mind of man. Its value lies in the fact that it does for the human race what no other science pretends to do: that is, to show us our proper place in life.

Horary astrology, so named from the Latin word *hora* (hour), comes closer to divination than any of the other branches. Built upon scientific principles, it is easily understood and most advantageous. All questions can be answered satisfactorily relating to past, present and future events.

A horary question, so called, is the birth chart of all the chief mental factors within the mind of the person; and in the chart will be found all the chief factors concerning this question, as focused in and mirrored upon the astral or thought plane.

The time the person first thinks seriously about the matter will be the exact birth hour of the question; the same as the exact birth hour is the birth of the physical body.

But unless this question is of very serious import, and asked at a time of most serious agitation over a really important human concern, it will be useless. So a horary chart should show us the proper procedure for a decision.

These astral or thought vibrations, impinging upon us, stimulate our mind, and in almost every case this horary chart will and does tie up with the person's own progressed natal chart because when the planets in the progressed or natal chart make favorable or unfavorable aspects, or when they come to an angular position, they strongly influence certain thoughts, which will eventually prove to be things. At least the thoughts will be stimulated or dominated by this particular question.

If the relations between the planets in the horary question tie up with the natal chart in any way, good or bad, the question will naturally have to be born; therefore, usually it is asked even if the person only asks himself.

It is much easier to answer this question through a horary chart than to read it correctly in a natal chart, because a natal chart is an exact science and a horary chart is essentially a chart of divination.

If a thought or a planetary vibration is strong enough to dominate the thinking brain of a person, it has arisen first on the astral plane where thoughts originate. And a trained reader can interpret the chart correctly in all its details, just like a photographer develops a picture.

The astrologer can, by carefully comparing the harmony or discord existing between the different factors seen to be involved in the matter asked about, interpret the nature of the true developments as associated with it and predict with certainty the result of any question.

Of course horary astrology bears out wonderfully the idea of celestial correspondence to mundane affairs.

It exemplifies the sympathy existing between the operations of the mind and the planetary vibrations, leading us to ask questions of importance at times when the progressions bear definite relations to the natal. Otherwise there could be no evolution and nothing would be gained through different experiences.

To become proficient in horary astrology , we must first become familiar with natal astrology, especially the casting of the horoscope, local time corrections, the nature of the signs, planets, houses and aspects.

I do not wish to infer that an astrologer must have a person's natal chart in order to read and interpret correctly a horary question. I am merely pointing out the relations between the question asked and the natal planetary vibrations.

But in some questions, such as those concerning surgery (when necessary), or questions of sickness, the natal chart should be studied in conjunction with the horary question. Suppose the question were asked, "Should I have an operation?" The astrologer should, by all means, consult the person's natal chart before predicting events of such serious and vital nature.

When we fully understand what a horary question consists of, we are right in refusing to answer certain questions. We will be more successful in answering questions correctly if we stay within the principles of this science. And, if we intend to keep astrology scientific, we must stay with its principles.

If we are earnestly endeavoring to analyze correctly and interpret a person's thought-question by the planetary configurations, our only concern is to interpret correctly the fundamental facts in the chart. It isn't whether we wish or would like to see a person do the thing about which he has asked. It is whether the chart says it is best for him to do so. Let us be honest and sincere regardless of personal feelings. The person may not like honest predictions, but in time will learn to respect and have confidence in the astrologer who is honest and just about the chart in question.

Working out a system of, shall we say, planetary bookkeeping, and staying strictly within certain astrological principles, the astrologer will find his predictions successful, and can answer any and all questions with certainly.

We should be very humble and thankful that we have this divine science to guide us, thus helping to keep us from unnecessary mistakes. Astrology or cosmic law is not in the least concerned with people Who do not believe it, or cannot understand its laws. The reason these people do not believe and understand is because they are mentally too indolent to study and learn.

Those who are fortunate enough to be able to investigate the wonderful scientific truths of astrology, have to delve deeply and study hard to find and prove these truths. Anyone with ordinary intelligence, coupled with lots of earnest, patient study will learn to understand and interpret these great truths. It is a life-long study because it is life.

The Sun, Moon and planets in their course are the most rhythmical of all nature's manifestations, regulating the temperature, the atmosphere, the tides and the human mind. Our history is cyclic and can be equally traced in the development of religion, in the rise and fall of nations, in politics and economics. Nothing is left to chance.

The work of the Creator must have been founded on a definite plan; and in our solar system the revolving planets are surely the wheels energized and spinning from the solar Sun, doing their part according to divine plan.

The Sun is the source of life on our planet, the earth; and likewise it must be the source of life on our sister planets.

The path of the earth in its travel through space around the Sun is constant. It travels the same track month after month, year after year, and century after century. It does so only as a result of the attracting and repelling, or magnetic and electric forces of the other planets. Let one stop in its course or deviate therefrom, and the proper balance would be lost, and our earth, more than likely, would fly off at a tangent. And if it missed colliding with one of the other equally controlled planets, it would disappear into the universal ether as a frozen mass.

This indeed teaches us a wonderful truth in regard to our individual personal life. For instance, it is easy for the man who is habitually truthful to tell the truth. It is easy for the moral man to live a moral life.

It is easy for us who think and study to keep on thinking and studying. These things may all be hard to do at first, but when the habit has been formed, it is just as hard to do otherwise.

The ancient belief that the planets were gods, who had under their special care the affairs of mankind, arose not from superstitution, but from observations of calamities accompanying or immediately following certain relative positions of the planets, Saturn and Mars, and the benefits attending upon similar positions of Jupiter and Venus.

It was by watching these planets' transits and the eclipses, especially to the major planets, that ancient astrologers foretold the nature of events about to happen, and named the countries most likely to be affected by them.

Quoting from Dr. Richard Garnet, one of our moderns, "Astrology, with the single exception of astronomy, is as regards the certainty of its data the most exact of all exact sciences."

Henry Ward Beecher, when asked his opinion of astrology, said, "I think its principles are sound, and the practical application of astrology should interest every human being."

Astronomy is the outgrowth of astrology. Astronomy is the scientific phase of casting a horoscope. Astrology is the key that unlocks these mathematical figures. Thus we may read the message, that God has written therein.

Astrology is the soul of astronomy.

Sir James Jeans, the great astronomer, tells us that around our Sun are millions and thirty thousands of millions of suns all shining with their own light. All astronomers speak of our universe as a tiny island universe, and of our earth as a very humble planet which is not shining with its own light, but with light borrowed from the Sun.

The yardstick used to measure distance in the universe is the distance that light travels per second. If we multiply one hundred and eighty-six thousand miles by sixty (for the minutes), multiply again by sixty (for the hours), multiply again the total by twenty-four (for the days),

multiply that total by three hundred and sixty-five (for the years) , then we may begin to realize how far light, life and love, the power of God, go in one year./

Most of us do not or will not measure anything but what we personally think. Life or the great Law does not care anything for us. We must care for it. We must reach up and search for it. It is too great to come down to us.

Through constant search and application we may be able to come into conscious communication with the higher realms through the study of astrology.

These truths are sealed until through normal growth we evolve to where we can control and utilize them. Our Bible tells us, "Know the truth and the truth shall set you free."

The power of deity itself is in equilibrium with its wisdom; hence the only results are harmony. The world is always in some cycle which is part of the divine plan. It naturally follows, of course, that human beings are likewise meeting these cycles.

If we do not know enough of the great law to be in harmony, then we fly off at a tangent. That is bad. And whom do we blame? That's a question.

In compiling this book on horary astrology, I wish to make clear to the student that horary astrology corresponds to matter, inasmuch as it relates to the physical life. It is used to answer all questions concerning our daily problems and affairs in general. It is interesting, fascinating, educational and practical.

Use it and convince yourself; that is my, the author's, wish.

Chart Components

The Zodiac

The zodiac is a great belt or circle 12° wide with the ecliptic passing through the middle of it. It contains the 12 signs of the zodiac, which formerly corresponded to the 12 constellations bearing the same names. Now, owing to the precession of the equinoxes, each constellation is in the sign that has the name next following its own. The following are the names of the signs in their order:

Spring	Autumn
♈ Aries, Ram	♎ Libra, Balance or Scales
♉ Taurus, Bull	♏ Scorpio, Scorpion
♊ Gemini, Twins	♐ Sagittarius, Archer
Summer	*Winter*
♋ Cancer, Crab	♑ Capricorn, Goat
♌ Leo, Lion	♒ Aquarius, Water-bearer
♍ Virgo, Virgin	♓ Pisces, Fishes

Aries, Taurus, Gemini, Cancer, Leo and Virgo are northern signs. Libra, Scorpio, Sagittarius, Capricorn, Aquarius and Pisces are southern signs. Aries and Libra are called the equinoctial signs because when the Sun passes through them the days and nights are equal. The Sun enters Aries on March 21, and Libra on September 21 every year.

Cancer and Capricorn are called tropical signs because they limit the course of the Sun, which, after it has arrived at their first points, seems to turn and diminish in declination, causing summer by the turn it makes in Cancer, and winter by the turn it makes in Capricorn.

The 22nd day of June is the longest day in the year, and the 22nd day of December is the shortest. The Sun enters Cancer on or about June 21 and reaches its highest point of north declination, 23°27', and remains in this declination for three days, apparently standing still, after which the Sun slowly starts, crablike, backward toward its south declination. This is the summer solstice.

The Sun is seen to come yearly to the lowest part of the great cross at the winter solstice in the sign Capricorn, reaching its lowest point in south declination, 23°37', on December 22, remaining in that degree for three days, after which on December 25, the Sun ascends like a new birth or resurrection. This 22nd day of December is the shortest day of the year.

Each of the signs contains 30° which when multiplied by the 12 signs gives 360°, this being the total number of degrees contained in the zodiac.

The Ten Planets

The ten bodies, called planets, and their symbols are:

♆ Neptune	♃ Jupiter	♀ Venus
♅ Uranus	♂ Mars	☿ Mercury
♄ Saturn	☉ Sun	☽ Moon
♀ Pluto		

The Asteroids

The asteroids are:

Vesta   Juno   Pallas   Ceres

There are other points which must be considered, viz.:

☊ The Dragon's Head, or Moon's North Node

☋ The Dragon's Tail, or Moon's South Node.

⊕ The Part of Fortune

The Moon's Nodes

The Dragon's Head, the North Node of the Moon, is where the Moon crosses the ecliptic into north latitude.

The Dragon's Head is to the Moon what the Sun is to the sign Aries—always good.

The Dragon's Tail, the South Node of the Moon, is where the Moon crosses the ecliptic into south latitude. The Dragon's Tail is to the Moon what the Sun is to the sign Libra. It diminishes the power of good and increases that of evil planets.

The Dragon's Head is the commencement. The Dragon's Tail is the dissolution. These Nodes are very important in all horary questions.

The Part of Fortune

The Part of Fortune indicates the source from which we may expect to gain. This gain will come from the sign it is in and its house position. The planet disposing of the Part of Fortune will help to answer certain questions of lost and mislaid articles.

The Part of Fortune is derived by adding the longitude of the Ascendant to the Moon's longitude, from which sum is subtracted the longitude of the Sun. The remainder will be the Part of Fortune, which is always as far away from the Ascendant as the Moon is from the Sun.

Example: Suppose the Ascendant is 7 Aquarius 46. That is 10 signs, 7 degrees and 46 minutes from the first point of Aries. The Moon is in 17 Aries 23, i.e., 0 signs, 17 degrees and 23 minutes from the first point of Aries. From the sum of these two we are to subtract the longitude of the Sun (which is in 11 Sagittarius 23), and the remainder will represent the number of signs, degrees and minutes that the Part of Fortune is from the first point of Aries.

Longitude of Ascendant	10 signs 7 degrees 46 minutes
Longitude of Moon	+ 0 signs 17 degrees 23 minutes
	10 signs 25 degrees 9 minutes
Longitude of Sun	− 8 signs 11 degrees 23 minutes
	2 signs 13 degrees 46 minutes

equals Gemini 13:46 as place of Part of Fortune.

The Aspects

Aspects denote action, and in all horary questions, things materialize and are brought about by aspect, and this aspect must be applying.

Parallel ∥—Planets are parallel when they are in the same degree of declination. The student should pay very particular attention to the declination of the planets, as the zodiacal parallel is of more importance than any other aspect. It is the same as a close conjunction but more powerful.

Conjunction ☌—Planets are in conjunction when they are in the same longitude. If they are exactly in the same degree and minute and sign, it is a partile conjunction, and very powerful.

Trine △—The trine aspect is a distance of four signs, or 120° in the zodiac. It is considered as the best aspect of all. It is formed according to the element represented by the signs.

Square □—The square aspect is a distance of three signs, or 90° apart and measures one-quarter of the circle of 360°, and is considered evil. Seldom can its malefic influence be lessened by the interposition of more friendly aspects.

Sextile ✶—The sextile is formed when the planets are two signs distant from each other, or 60° apart, and is very benefic, meaning opportunity.

Opposition ☍—The opposition is when two planets are 180° distant, or half the space in the zodiac, which places them in diametrical radiation. It is considered an evil and unfortunate aspect in all horary questions.

The Effect of the Aspects

There are many other aspects, but they are of no importance in a horary question. Allow an orb of 6° for the Sun and planets. But allow the Moon the full orb of its last application to a planet, or to the Ascendant, as this is usually what the result will be, as the Moon materializes what the Sun and planets promise.

The trine aspect brings things to pass with ease and will prove most beneficial.

The sextile will bring things to pass if the opportunity is grasped as once. But if this aspect happens from cadent houses, usually nothing is done about it. However, the sextile can and will bring things to pass without any difficulty. The opportunity is there for the thing to materialize.

The opposition sometimes brings things to pass; more often it does not. This would depend entirely on the kind of question asked, and the houses from which the aspect happens. In a horary question, the opposition aspect denotes envy, jealousy and enmity. If the matter inquired about ever does transpire, whichever ruler is the weakest by sign or by house denotes which person or thing will suffer most.

The square aspect frequently brings things to pass, especially if it is from the angles. But so many obstacles, and so much difficulty will be experienced that it is best left alone. There is too much doubt and suspicion connected with this aspect for any good to materialize. If this aspect happens in succedent or cadent houses, it will not transpire.

Terms Used in Horary Astrology

Mutual Reception is a strong testimony that the thing inquired about will transpire, but is not strong enough when used alone. Mutual reception is when two planets are mutually posited in each other's signs.

Example: The planet Venus rules the signs Libra and Taurus. The planet Uranus rules the sign Aquarius. Should Venus be in Aquarius and Uranus be in Taurus at any time, these two planets would be in mutual reception by sign position.

There can be mutual reception by trine, by square, or by opposition. Venus in Aquarius and Uranus in Libra is mutual reception by trine. Venus in Aquarius and Uranus in Taurus is mutual reception by square.

Venus in Aries and Mars in Libra is mutual reception by opposition. In case of mutual reception by square or opposition, the mutual reception is stronger than the evil aspect and helps to mitigate its evil. These are powerful aspects and very important in any chart.

In horary questions, if the ruler of the question inquired about is *retrograde*, the matter, if it does transpire, will never be all that is promised or expected. Suppose the rulers of a question are forming an aspect, and before the aspect is completed, one of the rulers turns retrograde. The person or thing signified by this retrograde planet will either change his mind or be hindered in some way, so that the matter will not be completed satisfactorily.

If before an aspect between the two rulers or the co-ruler is completed, one of the rulers passes into another sign, it shows some change has taken place in the affair. This is important in all questions of misplaced or hidden articles.

Translation of Light is a strong aspect to bring things to pass, and many times this one aspect alone will do so. This happens when the chief rulers of the question are separating from an aspect with each other, and another planet, faster moving, aspects first one of them, and immediately aspects the other, translating the light from one to the other.

This third planet, the one that translates, shows that the matter will be brought about by a third party, or a helpful circumstance.

Suppose, for example, that we have two rulers separating from an aspect to each other, and Mercury aspects first one ruler, then immediately aspects the other. We would say the matter would be brought to perfection by the third or sixth house influence. It could be a letter, neighbor or relative, or whatever the third house would promise, depending on the kind of question.

Of course, the Moon is the most powerful translator of light, as the Moon is always co-ruler of every question. This is most powerful for bringing things to pass quickly.

Collection of Light brings things to perfection. This happens when the two rulers of the question do not make any aspect to each other, but both of them make an aspect to a more weighty planet than themselves. The planet that they both aspect will be the means of bringing the thing to perfection.

Many times we see two people at a standstill, or not in harmony, and a friend or another person is able to help reconcile all difficulties. This would be a most important aspect in all law questions.

Take, for example, Jupiter gradually leaving Saturn, and both eventually making a trine to Neptune in Virgo. Neptune is thus the reconciler of many differences of opinion, etc.

I advise the student to use and study the translation and collection of light in all horary questions. They are two of the strongest aspects to bring things to pass.

A planet is said to be peregrine when it is placed in a sign where it has no dignity, and it is considered a negative answer to the question. Especially is this important in questions of theft, as a peregrine planet in any angle, or in the second house, denotes the thief. However, no planet is reckoned peregrine when it is in mutual reception.

Suppose Venus were in Aries where it has no dignity. Venus is said to be in her detriment in Aries. Mars in Taurus is in his detriment. But with Venus in Mars' sign and Mars in Venus' sign, they would not be peregrine because they would be in mutual reception.

Uranus in Leo and the Sun in Aquarius would be another example; Venus in Scorpio and Mars in Taurus is another.

A *combust* planet means any planet 8 degrees and 30 minutes before or after the Sun's body, but these planets must be in the same sign the Sun occupies when the question is asked.

This signifies a negative answer to any question unless the Sun is chief ruler of the rising sign or rules the sign of the question under consideration.

If the Sun is the ruler of the Ascendant or house ruling the question, this aspect should not be considered combust unless the planet or planets making or leaving the 8 degree and 30 minute aspect of the Sun's body are in their detriment or badly aspected.

Only the Moon, Venus and Mercury can aspect the Sun in horary questions. These planets are not considered as malefics, unless it would be the planet Mercury which is convertible.

If these planets are not badly aspected to the malefics when in the combust way, they should be read as hastening to or leaving the conjunction or translating the light to the Sun which is considered a powerful aspect in any chart; otherwise a combust planet signifies a negative answer to any question.

Via Combust or the *Combust Way* is when any planet is in the last 15 degrees of the sign Libra to the first 15 degrees of the sign Scorpio.

It is so-called because of violent fixed stars being there and is said to render the planets in these degrees and signs unfortunate, especially the Moon who suffers as much as during an eclipse.

Here again we must make an exception; any planet within 1 degree orb or exactly conjunct the fixed star Spica, which is in 22 Libra 27, is considered most fortunate, meaning honor and fame, so do not consider a planet or planets in this degree Via Combust.

If the Moon, Venus or Mercury should be in these Via Combust degrees and signs and in the exact combust way of the Sun, the question would be considered extremely unfortunate and the conditions critical.

A planet is considered Under the Sunbeams when it is less than 17 degrees from the Sun's body and is considered in a horary question as fear, trouble and oppression but not so bad as combust—so the text books say.

However, I have not found this to be true unless these planets are badly aspected, and, as all aspects in horary questions must be read as applying, again we must consider the applying planets as Moon, Mercury and Venus to the Sun.

So unless these planets were applying to a bad aspect of malefics when under the Sun's beams, I could not consider this 17 degree orb of the Sun as negative.

However the astrologer or student should prove these rules through much research and study. Each question at the birth hour is just as different as the individual natal chart and should be judged and read accordingly.

The Measure of Time		
Angular Houses	*Succedent Houses*	*Cadent Houses*
Movable signs on the angles Give days	Movable signs on succedent house Give weeks	Movable signs on cadent house Give months
Common signs on the angles Give weeks	Common signs on succedent house Give months	Common signs on cadent house Give years
Fixed signs on the angles Give months	Fixed signs on succedent house Give years	Fixed signs on cadent house Unknown time

The planet that makes the aspect by application is what brings things to pass. If in cardinal signs, quick action; in common signs, after a reasonable time; and in fixed signs, after much delay.

Always remember that planets increasing in light and motion bring things to pass more quickly. The time it would take the matter to transpire would be the difference in the degrees between the rulers of the question, and the signs and houses they occupy.

It is very difficult to judge time correctly, but it can be done accurately. Time is judged by house position of planets, the sign they occupy, and by the aspect applying.

The degrees between the body or aspect of the rulers, according to the number of degrees, determine the number of hours, days, weeks, months or years it will be before the matter inquired about is accomplished or destroyed.

In all questions of hidden, misplaced or stolen articles, wherever the ruler is, there is the thing. And the house where the ruler of the thing is posited shows the quarter of the heavens or point of the compass where the thing may be. It is therefore necessary to know the directions of the houses and also the directions of the signs in order to find where things are, and to locate persons.

The Directions by Houses		
Houses	*Houses*	*Houses*
First, East	Fifth, North by West	Ninth, Southwest
Second, North by East	Sixth, West Northwest	Tenth, South
Third, Northeast	Seventh, West	Eleventh, Southeast by South
Fourth, North	Eighth, West by South	Twelfth, East Southeast

The Directions by Signs		
Aries, East	Leo, East by North	Sagittarius East by South
Taurus, South by East	Virgo, South by West	Capricorn, South
Gemini, West by South	Libra, West	Aquarius, West by North
Cancer, North	Scorpio, North by East	Pisces, North by West

In all questions of hidden, misplaced or stolen articles, wherever the ruler is, there is the thing. And the house where the ruler of the thing is posited shows the quarter of the heavens or point of the compass where the thing may be. It is therefore necessary to know the directions of the houses and also the directions of the signs in order to find where things are, and to locate persons.

The Twelve Departments of Life

All events and affairs are represented by the 12 houses of the chart. All questions must therefore relate to one or more of these 12 departments of life. It is absolutely essential to determine to which house a question belongs. Weigh each question carefully to determine the thing inquired about.

Suppose, for example, that the question is about business. That is a tenth house question. But first find out if it relates more to honor, power, authority, or to the actual revenue derived from the business.

If the person who asks the question is concerned about promotion, or a situation, it would be strictly a tenth house question. Should it be about money derived from business, or in any way about wages, we would have to consider the eleventh house, as the eleventh is the second from the tenth, and therefore the money involved.

Just as the first house is always the querent and the second his money or personal belongings, so the seventh house is other people and the eighth is their money. We must use the right house pertaining to the question if a correct answer and judgment is to be given.

All the houses are distinguished by figures and are either angular, as Aries, east; Capricorn, south; Libra, west; and Cancer, north; or by first, tenth, seventh and fourth houses.

The succedent houses are the second, fifth, eighth and eleventh.

Cadent houses are third, sixth, ninth and twelfth.

The Sun rises in the east Aries at 6:00 a.m. At noon the Sun is on the Meridian. The Sun sets in the west Libra at 6:00 p.m. over the western angle, or Descendant. At the north the Sun is on the Nadir, or midnight, being the opposite point the Sun possesses at noon.

Angular houses have the greatest power; next, the succedent; and last, the cadent houses. The houses are based on the Sun's position at the time of a birth or the hour of any question under consideration. The position of the Sun proves whether the chart is correct or otherwise. So the time is the important factor in casting a horoscope.

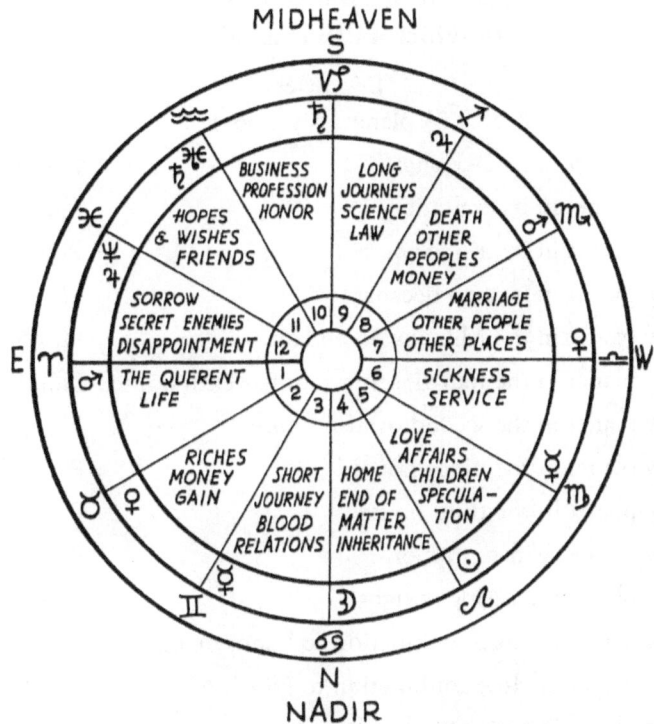

A Diagram Explaining the Significations of the Twelve Houses of the Heavens and Planets Ruling These Heavens

Dignities and Debilities of Planets

In working with horary questions I have used with much success the table to determine the degrees to which a planet is affected. Many of the writers give these tables. Any student can compile the same from Simonite's *Arcana of Astrology* under the heading of Definitions of Terms. I have added a few of my own, as you will see when you use it.

These are very important and useful in questions where the good and negative aspects of the questions seem evenly blended, and therefore make it difficult to come to any decision. This table will, if used exactly as set forth, give the decision correctly.

Table to Determine the Degrees to Which a Planet is Affected

Dignities
(A planet may enjoy)

Any planet in its own sign	Plus 5
Any planet in its exaltation	Plus 4
Any planet in its triplicity	Plus 3
Any planet in its own decanate	Plus 1
Any planet in the M.C. or Ascendant	Plus 5
Any planet in the fourth, seventh or eleventh house	Plus 4
Any planet in the second or fifth house	Plus 3
Any planet in the ninth house	Plus 2
Any planet in the third house	Plus 1
Any planet swift in motion	Plus 4
Any planet increasing in light	Plus 3
Any planet in close conjunction to Venus or Jupiter	Plus 5
Any planet in close conjunction to North Node	Plus 5
Any planet in trine aspect to Venus or Jupiter	Plus 4
Any planet in conjunction to fixed star Spica	Plus 5
(Spica 22° ♎ 27' denotes fame, honor)	
Any planet in mutual reception	Plus 4

Debilities
A planet may suffer)

Any planet in its detriment	Minus 5
Any planet in its fall	Minus 4
Any planet peregrine (when not in mutual reception)	Minus 5
Any planet in the twelfth house	Minus 5
Any planet in the sixth or eighth house	Minus 2
Any planet retrograde	Minus 5

Any planet slow in motion	Minus 2
Any planet decreasing in light	Minus 3
Any planet combust	Minus 5
Any planet in exact conjunction to Saturn or Mars	Minus 4
Any planet conjunct South Node	Minus 3
Any planet square or opposition to Saturn or Mars	Minus 4
Any planet within 5° of Caput Algol	Minus 5
(Caput Algol 25° ♉ 10'—most evil star in heavens	
Any planet Via Combust (15° ♎ to 15° ♏)	Minus 5
But if in 22° ♎ with Spica, count	Plus 5
Any planet Under the Sun Beams	Minus 4

I use this as horary bookkeeping. Suppose a horary question has many aspects for a favorable answer, and at the same time there are negative aspects so that the astrologer is at a loss to make a definite statement.

Use this table, and it will answer the question in this way.

Suppose there were 15 points for dignities the planets would enjoy and 10 points for the debilities the planets would suffer.

There would be five points in favor of the question. So I would decide that it would materialize and be beneficial for the querent. If there were 15 debilities and 10 dignities I would decide against it. This is most interesting to use also in natal charts.

Countries and Cities Ruled by the Zodiacal Signs

Aries—England, Germany, Lower Poland, Japan, Palestine, Denmark. Cities and towns: Birmingham, Naples, Florence, Verona, Marseilles.

Taurus—Asia Minor, Ireland, Persia, White Russia (Belarus), Holland, Grecian Archipelago. Cities and towns: St. Louis, Dublin, Mantua, Leipzig.

Gemini—United States, Belgium, Flanders, Wales, Lower Egypt, West of England. Cities and towns: London, Plymouth, San Francisco, Versailles, Nuremberg.

Cancer—Scotland, North and West Africa, Zealand, Paraguay. Cities and towns: Manchester, Algiers, New York, Istanbul, Venice, Milan, Amsterdam, Stockholm.

Leo—Italy, Sicily, France, Bohemia, Northern Romania. Cities and towns: Chicago, Philadelphia, Rome, Bath, Bombay, Portsmouth, Bristol, Damascus.

Virgo—Greece, West Indies, Turkey, Babylonia, Switzerland, Brazil, and the country between the Tigris and Euphrates rivers. Cities and towns: Los Angeles, Boston, Paris, Heidelberg, Bagdad, Jerusalem.

Libra—Tibet, Upper Egypt, Japan, Argentina, Austria, northern China, Indochina, Burma. Cities and towns: Leeds, Frankfort, Antwerp, Copenhagen, Lisbon, Vienna, Johannesburg, Charleston.

Scorpio—Norway, Morocco, Judea, Algeria, Syria, Jutland, Queensland. Cities and towns: New Orleans, Baltimore, Washington, DC, Cincinnati, Milwaukee, Halifax, Newcastle, Dover.

Sagittarius—Arabia, Italy and France (parts of each), Spain, Hungary, Provence, Australia. Cities and towns: Cologne, Stuttgart, Nottingham, Sheffield, Avignon, Toledo.

Capricorn—Bosnia, Bulgaria, Albania, Macedonia, Mexico, India, Afghanistan. Cities and towns: Port Said, Brussels, Oxford, Constanz.

Aquarius—Red Russia, Arabia, Sweden, Prussia, Lithuania, part of Poland, Abyssinia, Piedmont. Cities and towns: Brighton, Salisbury, Trent, Bremen, Hamburg.

Pisces—Normandy, Sahara Desert, Portugal, Egypt and the southern part of Asia Minor. Cities and towns: Lancaster, Ratisbon, Alexandria, Seville.

About Colors

It is interesting, and in some questions necessary, to know color descriptions of the signs and planets.

Colors Ruled by the Planets

Uranus—plaids, checks and mingled colors.
Saturn—black and green.
Jupiter—red mixed with green, or ash colored.
Mars—fiery red or scarlet.
Sun—yellow, inclined to purple.
Venus—white and purple, bluish.
Mercury—light blue, azure, or dove color.
Moon—white or light spotted cream color.

Compound Signification

Uranus and Saturn—green plaids.
Uranus and Jupiter—green and red plaids.
Uranus and Mars—red plaids.
Uranus and Sun—green and purple plaids.
Uranus and Venus—blue and white plaids.
Uranus and Mercury—light blue plaids.
Uranus and Moon—fine checked plaids.
Saturn and Jupiter—dark green spotted with dark.
Saturn and Mars—dark reddish-brown, tawny.
Saturn and Sun—a blackish-orange and shining, bronze.
Saturn and Venus—a light gray.
Saturn and Mercury—a dark blue or gray.
Saturn and Moon—a deep russet or gray.
Jupiter and Mars—a tawny, light-spotted.
Jupiter and Venus—a greenish-gray.

Jupiter and Mercury—a spotted green.
Jupiter and Moon—a high-colored green.
Mars and Sun—a deep red or scarlet.
Mars and Venus—light red or crimson.
Mars and Mercury—a tawny red or brick color.
Mars and Moon—a light red and glistening.
Sun and Venus—olive color.
Sun and Mercury—light gray, blue gray.
Sun and Moon—light yellow or green.
Venus and Mercury—purple or light mixture.
Venus and Moon—light blue or bluish-white.
Mercury and Moon—buff or fawn color.

Colors of the Zodiacal Signs

Aries—white mixed with red.
Taurus—white mixed with lemon.
Gemini—white mixed with crimson.
Cancer—green or russet.
Leo—red or green.
Virgo—black, speckled.
Libra—black, or dark crimson, or tawny color.
Scorpio—brown.
Sagittarius—yellow, or green sanguine.
Capricorn—black, or russet, or a swarthy brown.
Aquarius—ashy color with blue.
Pisces—white glistening color.

Suppose the ruler is Saturn in the tenth house, in the sign Capricorn, in no close aspect to any other planet. We could safely say all black; if Saturn were in the sign Leo, that would add green or red, as mixing the planets in different signs gives different colors.

Planets in conjunction also give different colors.

Anyone with a strong Uranus in his or her chart loves colors. If Uranus aspects Venus, the individual loves pastel shades, etc. Whenever the major planets enter the different signs, color schemes change. With Uranus' entrance into Taurus, we had a variety of colors, two tones, and brilliant shades. We had two tones in furniture, automobiles, streamlined trains, etc. When this planet entered Gemini we had lighter shades—light blue, azure tones and white mixed with all the light colors.

Neptune entering Virgo gave us beautiful materials. Mercury, ruler of Virgo, rules merchandise. When Neptune was last in this sign we had a revolution in merchandise of all kinds and descriptions.

Venus rules Taurus, and Venus rules, among many other things, millinery shops and salons. When Uranus enters this sign, an increased number of people patronize salons and shop for hats.

Uranus in Taurus has given some beautiful creations in wraparounds, turbans, brilliant handkerchiefs, and costume jewelry. We could write pages and never exhaust the interesting study of colors, so fascinating is this study of the planets and signs ruling the various colors.

In all cases of healing, color plays an important part. Investigation by scientists brings to light the fact that the chemical rays of the Sun, when analyzed through various colored glasses, are of powerful use in the healing of skin and other diseases. These rays of the Sun, when analyzed through the spectrum, exhibit seven colors, and these colors correspond to the seven planets. Each of the colors corresponds to a tone on the musical scale.

Water kept in colored glass bottles and subjected to the rays of the Sun will gain chemical properties. Red, being a stimulating color, would act as a tonic; blue as a nerve stimulant; yellow as an opening medicine; purple for blood and liver disorders; green for inflamed eyes; blue for weak eyes; orange to whet the appetite; and yellow also acts as a remedy for bowel trouble. All this and much, much more makes the study of colors fascinating and educational.

The Kinds of Employment Ruled by Each Planet

The planet oriental to the Sun usually gives the key to the vocation or work. The nativity must be studied in its entirety to determine the ability of the person. The higher the organic quality, the higher the type, all things being equal. The positive type represents the highly organized qualities. The negative type reflects disorganization that results from the inability of the person to control circumstances.

The dignities and the debilities a planet may enjoy and suffer should be studied. A sequence of planets is very powerful for attainment. Planets occupying positive and negative signs are most important. Starting with the first sign of the zodiac, the sign Aries, every other sign is positive; so every second sign in the zodiac from the positive sign is negative. The more planets that occupy positive signs, the more positive that person will be.

There are only three positive electric planets: Jupiter, Mars and Sun, unless we include Pluto, which I am inclined to do. If Pluto is the higher octave of Mars, it would then, as I see it, be a positive planetary vibration.

It is possible for an individual, highly organized, to respond to the higher vibrations of the planets at any time. The study of the characteristics common to each individual is the starting point for a more common comprehensive conception of the Universe as a whole. The subject and object of our every conclusion should be humanity. Astrology holds the keys to unlock the doors or centers of knowledge that we may learn life's laws and lessons.

Neptune gives bootleggers, kidnapers, music composers, photographers, caricaturists, speculators, diplomats, politicians, mediums.

Uranus gives astrologers, chemists, metaphysicians, designers, occultists, legislators, interpreters, aviators, salespeople, orators, radio broadcasters, telegraphers, auto mechanics, and all occupations connected with the air and with communication.

Saturn gives coal miners, farmers, brick masons, priests, timekeepers, undertakers, pottery workers, tailors, magicians, shoemakers, tanners.

Jupiter gives judges, ambassadors, bishops, bankers, cashiers, gamblers, golfers, lawyers, clothiers, preachers, professors, doctors.

Mars gives farmers, carpenters, reporters, mechanics, adventurers, railway workers, law enforcers, barbers, insurance agents, butchers, dentists, firemen, generals, surgeons, soldiers.

Sun gives kings, emperors, lieutenants, justices of the peace, managers, athletes, adjustment commissioners, employers, executives, ambassadors.

Venus gives dressmakers, entertainers, florists, hair dressers, milliners, musicians, perfumers, linen drapers, painters, tailors, nursery employees, artists, actors, poets, librarians, cooks, needle workers, dramatic readers.

Mercury gives accountants, architects, astronomers, bookkeepers, clerks, grocers, mail carriers, merchants, messengers, printers, publishers, secretaries, stationers, stenographers, stool pigeons, store keepers, tennis players, acousticians, essayists, statisticians, mental healers, inventors, teachers, thieves, servants.

Moon gives sailors, travelers, brewers, milkmen, coachmen, marines, millers, boatmen, dealers in fluids, nurses, bar maids, glass blowers, grocers, janitors, laundry employees, naval officers, silversmiths, waiters, vocalists, instrument tuners, stock breeders, etchers, unionists, welfare workers, naturopaths, governesses, merchant marines, mediums, valets, divers, employment agents, relief commissioners.

Planets in Business

Neptune rules the oil industry, fishing industry, hospitals, all charitable institutions and trusts.

Uranus rules railroads, electrical industries, aviation schools, and all businesses where communications gear is used and sold.

Saturn rules farming, mining, real estate, cement, sand, gravel, stocks and bonds, and banking.

Jupiter rules the religious and financial worlds.

Mars rules manufacturing and the building industries.

Sun rules government.

Venus rules entertainment, social functions, and political scheming.

Mercury rules schools, intellectual affairs, and publications.

Moon rules grocery stores, common employment, and retail stores.

Of course all divisions are subject to sub-division, and in turn ruled by all the planets. Each of the planets has rulership over a day of the week.

Sun rules Sunday, the hour of sunrise on that day, and also the 8th, 15th, and 22nd hours of the day.

Moon rules Monday, the hour of sunrise on that day and also the 8th, 15th, and 22nd hours of the day.

Mars rules Tuesday, the hour of sunrise on that day, and also the 8th, 15th, and 22nd hours of that day.

Mercury rules Wednesday, the hour of sunrise on that day and the 8th, 15th, and 22nd hours of that day.

Jupiter rules Thursday, the hour of sunrise on that day and the 8th, 15th, and 22nd hours of that day.

Venus rules Friday, the hour of sunrise on that day and the 8th, 15th, and 22nd hours of that day.

Saturn rules Saturday, the hour of sunrise on that day and the 8th, 15th, and 22nd hours of that day.

Uranus and *Neptune* are the octaves of Mercury and Venus, respectively, and the influence of these two planets will express on the days ruled by Mercury and Venus.

If the planet *Pluto* is the octave of the planet Mars, as most astrologers believe, we might watch Pluto's influence on Tuesday, the day ruled by Mars.

The Moon's Power

The Moon passing through the 12 signs takes on the character of each planet that rules the sign in which it happens to be. In Aries it is martial and masculine, or takes on the nature of the planet Mars. In Taurus it is negative and feminine, and takes on the character of Venus. The Moon is powerful in the sign Taurus because this is where the Moon is exalted. Apply this law to each sign the Moon happens to be in.

Well dignified in an angular house, with good aspects to the Sun, Jupiter or Venus, the pathway of life is brilliant, happy and successful, for under these aspects the Moon brings the good things of this world. The Moon's greatest enemy among the planets is Mars. When in bad aspect to this planet, it will have a bad effect on the health and brain. A bad aspect to Saturn is also bad for health, especially during the first seven years of life; and in later years, with bad aspects or transits, it again brings misfortunes.

When the Moon is badly aspected at birth, it makes the person temperamentally lazy, especially when in bad aspect to Venus or Neptune. These aspects cause neglect, and one could be very untidy or careless along certain lines. If Mars adds to these its evil aspect, there will be a tendency to drink or dissipation. The bad aspect to Mercury brings untruthfulness.

But the Moon in good aspect to Mercury strengthens the mind and gives mental energy; this is the best and strongest aspect for a clever intellect. With Venus also adding a good aspect there will be talent for music and fine arts.

The Moon in a cardinal sign (Aries, Cancer, Libra or Capricorn) leads one out into the great highroad of life, but unless she is fortified with strong benefic aspects of the Sun or other planets, there will be danger of misfortune, as one will lack continuity and strength of purpose. The Moon in good aspect to Saturn is of great help, giving caution and discrimination.

In fixed signs (Taurus, Leo, Scorpio or Aquarius) the Moon inclines the person to be patient, prudent, just, constant and enduring; sometimes obstinate, stubborn and avaricious.

In the common signs, Gemini, Sagittarius and Pisces, the Moon will make the person impressionable, changeable, wavering, adaptable, careless, fond of music and the arts but inclined to duplicity. In the common sign Virgo, she makes one ingenious, but inconstant. Of course, we must make our final decision from a blending of the whole chart.

The Sun and Moon are very important planets, whatever sign or house they are in. Next in importance is the ruler of the rising sign. A planet in the first house is one coming into power.

The ruler of the sign on the Ascendant, with the planet or planets in the first house, is the ruler of the horoscope. If there is more than one planet in this house, the one nearest the degree of this rising sign will be the ruler. The rest of them will be co-rulers. This is true of all nativities.

The Moon as Significator and Some Important Considerations

Always observe the aspect the Moon has just left, and also from what planet and aspect the ruler of the rising sign has separated, whether good or evil. This will show what has already taken place, according to the signs and houses in which they formed these aspects.

Their next applications will show what to expect, and the last aspect the Moon makes in the chart will determine the outcome of the matter.

In order for the question to be radical and fit to be judged, the Moon must make an aspect before it leaves the sign it is in, when the question is asked. If the Moon makes no aspect before it leaves the sign, (probably) nothing will come of the question except a lot of talk.

Use the Moon to make your decision regarding all questions of a complex nature, rather than try to go into detail, unless you have had years of experience. The Moon is the ruler and co-ruler in all questions.

We must try to learn everything possible regarding the influence of the planets, and bear in mind that each general division is susceptible to subdivision. But the Moon is the only planet in horary questions that is ruler and co-ruler of all these generalities. And if the Moon is applying to an aspect, good or bad, that is what will happen.

There is no other branch of astrology so rich in detail as this branch of the study, and it will help to understand and read a natal chart better, always with the thought in mind of the difference between the two kinds of charts.

Suppose when a person is born the planet Mars is ruler of the rising sign. That person would be aggressive, and to a certain extent argumentative at all times. But in a horary chart, should Mars be the ruler, it would show that the querent was in an argumentative frame of mind when he asked the question.

It is most important, if we wish to be proficient in our work, to bear in mind the natural zodiac when reading all charts. Whatever the sign on the Ascendant at birth, it is still the brain. Whatever the sign on the cusp of the third house, it is still that part of the intellect under the rulership of Mercury and the sign Gemini. This will give us a better understanding of the different planets in the different houses and signs. Therefore we may read with more intelligence.

Our intellect is our contact with principles (Gemini). This is, or should be, used in our contact with other people (Libra), and our intelligent selection of what or whom we cultivate (Aquarius), as these three air signs have to do with the intellect. The third, seventh and eleventh houses are the relative houses. The third house is blood relations; the seventh house our relations with other people; and the eleventh our social or mental relations.

Personal Description of the Twelve Signs and Planets in the Signs and the Disposition Produced by the Planets

The sign rising at the time of birth or at the time of a question, with no planet in the sign, should be studied by that rising sign, the ruler of it, by the sign this ruler is in, its house position and its aspects, and also the ruler of the decanate of the rising sign, because each sign contains three divisions of ten degrees each, called decanates, and each of these divisions is ruled by a different planet.

Each sign has a definite planet that rules the sign as a whole, but this sign also has as co-rulers, the planets that rule the other two signs of the same triplicity.

The sign *Aries* governs the head and is called the sign of the thinker; it is ruled by the planet Mars with the Sun and Jupiter, rulers of the second and third fiery signs, as co-rulers.

The first ten degrees of the sign *Aries* would therefore express all the dominant, pushing, combative tendencies of the planet Mars.

The second ten degrees, or from ten to twenty degrees, brings in the influence of the Sun, which is a great help as this is the sign of the Sun's exaltation, the thinker, being more conscious of the will, coordinates the mind and heart principles.

The third ten degrees, or from twenty to thirty degrees, brings in the influence of Jupiter, which mitigates the aggressiveness of Mars and leads toward religion and philosophy; this decanate, however, is not as beneficial as the Sun decanate. The second decanate of each sign is considered the best and strongest. Each of the signs should be studied by decanate and planet co-rulership.

Aries rising gives a strong body; medium stature; a head broad at the temples; ruddy complexion; sharp, expressive grey or grey-brown eyes; brown hair. This is a *motive mental* temperament.

Mars in Aries indicates one of medium stature; large boned, wiry body; long, oval face with a broad, furrowed forehead and high cheek bones; the ears are set high on the head and stand out from the face; long nose with dilated nostrils; the eyes deep-set, either red-brown, hazel-grey, or steel blue; the hair varies from sandy or reddish to dark; small mouth with full lips turning up at the corners; skin harsh, dry and freckled.

The disposition of the person with Mars in Aries is hasty, enthusiastic, jealous of honor, confident in his own powers, of great courage. He is the initiator of action and whatever is desired in life must be obtained by his own energy; learning by experience and not by advice, and naturally delights in argument or contention. When Mars is afflicted in Aries he is prone to violence, possesses not enough virtue and too much false pride, and is often treacherous and cruel.

For *Neptune* in *Aries*, see *Venus*.

Uranus in *Aries* may add to the height and thinness of the body, add more color to the skin and darken the eyes; the hair will be auburn.

In disposition these people are difficult to understand; they are originators of new methods and can improve upon the old, and are very eccentric. Moreover, they are not very fortunate unless Uranus is well aspected. Uranus in Aries gives sudden changes, fondness for machinery and electrical devices, mechanical ingenuity, and a love of travel. People with Uranus in Aries usually have a temper, are blunt and radical in speech and manner. They usually do not marry early in life and are not the best of marriage companions.

Saturn in *Aries* makes the body more bony and gives a long, thin face, bad teeth, eyes deep-set, small and close to the nose; thin lips, compressed and drooping at the corners; dark skin; a discontented expression.

In disposition he is crafty, boastful, difficult to understand, fond of dispute and arguing in which he is usually the conqueror, and never content. He requires discipline and careful training to bring out his best qualities. When Saturn is well aspected the person is very reserved, grave, patient, studious, solicitous, and a true friend except when unduly influenced by someone else which seldom occurs.

Jupiter in *Aries* lightens the hair to chestnut brown and adds some flesh or weight to the body, the head is well-shaped with a broad brow; the eyes large and kindly, either blue or grey-blue; the nose well-formed but inclined to be fleshy at the end; the mouth large, the teeth good, the chin prominent with a dimple in the center; the complexion fresh, sometimes tanned or brown.

When Jupiter in Aries is well aspected the person is a lover of peace and fair dealing, is kind, thoughtful, honorable, aspiring, idealistic, indulgent to his family, and liberal. Jupiter afflicted in Aries makes one deceptive and easily deceived, boastful of what he does not have, hypocritical and obstinate in maintaining false impressions, abusive and desirous of getting all he can without giving anything himself.

Sun in *Aries* gives medium height with broad shoulders; fair skin with a good deal of color in it; well-rounded forehead which the person wrinkles when he talks or studies; the hair is reddish-gold or light brown with red glints; the hair falls out early in life and the native becomes bald. The eyelashes and eyebrows are darker that the hair; the eyes golden-brown or hazel-green and very large.

The *Sun* is exalted in Aries and when well aspected here the disposition is noble and proud with lofty ideals, much human kindness; faithful, disinterested friend and a generous enemy; a natural leader, never easily discouraged, a lover of freedom and a possessor of much will power. He is extremely careful of and concerned over his personal appearance. When the Sun is afflicted in Aries he is proud and mean, talks a great deal, is restless, boastful, without judgment and selfish, a spendthrift and gambler, disliked because of his arrogance and ignorance.

Venus or *Neptune* in *Aries* shows one of medium stature with a slender, well-made, good-looking body; the hair is soft and thick; eyebrows marked in a long, sweeping, delicate line; eyes wide apart, dreamy and either a deep blue or brown; nose straight and short with flexible round nostrils; lips full with lots of color in them and the mouth beautiful; a dimple in the cheek or chin and sometimes a mark or scar on the face or neck.

In disposition even tempered, graceful, of charming manner, gracious, lovely, loving and well-beloved, appreciative of affection. When Venus is badly aspected in Aries the person is jealous, sensual, shameless, timid, given to all kinds of disgraceful actions and habits.

Mercury in *Aries* gives a thin body of medium height; graceful carriage; long face with a pointed chin; high forehead prominent at the temples; mobile features; straight nose, probably turned up at the tip; sensitive nostrils; eyes a little sunken and small but wide-open and expressive, hazel-grey or green-blue; long, thin, flexible lips; mouth slightly open, for these people are fluent, eloquent speakers, amusing and witty; a good clear skin and lots of brown hair.

In disposition Mercury in Aries gives an alert, keen, excitable person of subtle brain and intellect, a searcher after truth and one curious of deeper knowledge; one who argues with learning and discretion and learns all things with ease.

When Mercury is afflicted in Aries the person is erratic, tale-bearing, boastful, untruthful, and a malicious, mischief maker with no sense of judgment, constant in nothing but harmful things, discontented and easily led astray.

Moon in *Aries* denotes one of plump, medium stature with a round head, good complexion, full cheeks, short nose rounded at the tip, light brown or blond hair, possibly flaxen colored.

In disposition this person is changeable, sensitive, intuitive, rather timid; loves peace, science, pleasure and ease, travel, and novelties of all kinds; has many irons in the fire.

When badly aspected Moon in Aries makes one lazy, idle, stupid, addicted to bad habits, self-indulgent, careless of personal habits, very discontented, and disliking all kinds of labor.

Taurus rising gives a short or medium stature and a square-made body inclined to plumpness; thick, short, neck; full, broad forehead; large, round, prominent eyes which are very expressive and usually brown in color; wide nose and mouth; swarthy complexion and dark brown hair which is nearly always wavy or curly.

Taurus people are slow to anger but retain their anger a long time; they are rather melancholy. This sign gives the *vital temperament*.

Venus in *Taurus* adds to the beauty of the native but inclines to fleshiness because of the tendency toward self-indulgence, but the body is well-made; face full of color, the hair luxurious, dark brown, the eyes dark and lovely, called dove eyes.

In disposition the native is mild tempered, sweet and obliging, of kind disposition and generally beloved by everyone. They make desirable companions.

Neptune in *Taurus* same as *Venus*.

Uranus in *Taurus* gives a well-built individual of medium stature but inclines toward stoutness; not so good-looking; bad complexion; eyes tend toward grey and the hair is darker.

In disposition these people possess extraordinary insight and intuition and undertake everything with an ardent zeal to succeed. They are strangely sensitive. When Uranus is badly aspected in Taurus they are obstinate, eccentric, wayward and secretive.

Saturn in *Taurus* describes one of awkward appearance, about middle height, with dark, lanky hair rough skin which may be sallow, and weak eyes; a bad carriage and a slow, ungraceful walk.

In disposition determined in action, plodding, prudent, hard working, and possesses deep powers of concentration; can be depended upon in any emergency. He is the builder on all planes. When Saturn is badly aspected in Taurus the person is suspicious, jealous and rebellious; keeps in a rut, commits crimes for revenge, expresses all forms of limitation, has poor judgment. Selfishness and self-interest are the dominant traits.

Jupiter in *Taurus* denotes one of middle height with a stout, well-made body, good constitution and broad shoulders; curly hair and large, expressive, soft brown eyes.

In disposition this person will be wise, discreet, humane, fond of the opposite sex, and desirous of money, of which he usually has plenty and with which he is very generous. If badly aspected, Jupiter in Taurus shows an individual too free in his affections, who wants all for himself regardless of other people's feelings, and who spends too much on pleasure and personal adornment.

Mars in *Taurus* gives one of middle stature with well-made, muscular body; ruddy complexion; rough, coarse red-brown hair; an oval face, probably with a scar on the face or neck.

In disposition this person will be energetic, impulsive, confident, self-centered. When badly aspected the individual will be extravagant, impulsive, abusive, treacherous and false; over-indulgent in all physical activities, especially sex; morals questionable. Mars in Taurus, badly aspected, causes poverty; therefore we usually find that gamblers and all games of chance come under Mars afflicted in Taurus.

Sun in *Taurus* denotes a thick, short, strong, well-made athletic body; dark complexion; broad or Roman nose; wide mouth.

In disposition, proud, easily hurt, very generous and loving; possessed of much self-esteem and will do or die.

When badly aspected Sun in Taurus makes the person love to argue, dispute and never admit that he is wrong; miserable when crossed, mean in action and very revengeful.

Mercury in *Taurus* indicates middle stature, well-made body; thick, short brown hair and lots of it; light brown or grey eyes which are very expressive.

In disposition, Mercury in Taurus gives one slow to make decisions; when once made they seldom need changing as the decisions are based on reason and judgment which makes them reliable. Mercury afflicted gives extremely stubborn, secretive, wayward and vindictive temperaments.

Moon in *Taurus* gives a corpulent, well-made body of middle height or less; pale, dull complexion with moles on the face or neck; brown or black wavy or curly hair.

The disposition is noble, mild, obliging, of good mentality, just in actions, will merit respect and may attain much success in life. Badly aspected he is lazy in habits and temperament, overindulgent, sarcastic, and will have trouble over personal affairs and trouble and sorrow in marriage.

Gemini rising gives medium height, slender and well-made body, graceful carriage; long neck and head; broad forehead; expressive, bright eyes either hazel, blue-grey or green-grey, light brown hair and lots of it; small mouth with thin, well-formed lips; long hands and fingers. This is the *motive mental* temperament.

Mercury in *Gemini* denotes a tall, upright body; thin features; up-turned nose; clear complexion with some color in it; brown or hazel-grey eyes; springy walk.

In disposition this person will have a clever, penetrating intellect, a remarkable memory and reliable judgment.

When badly aspected he will be scatter-brained, tricky, nervous, ungrateful, unsympathetic and self-interested.

Uranus in *Gemini* gives a tall, well-made body; dull complexion; brown or dark eyes; dark brown hair; oval face; very intelligent looking.

In disposition, blunt, prompt, scientific but not always profound. This person could be successful in literature or science and is an eloquent orator.

If badly aspected the individual will express badly, be boasting, and quarrelsome, and too changeable to accomplish much. The mind is over-excitable. Accidents cause delay in education.

Saturn in *Gemini* denotes one of tall stature, slender but big-boned; dark complexion; dark brown or black hair; a serious look.

In disposition Saturn in Gemini shows independence, profound opinions, tact, quick perceptions, a good student. Badly aspected the person is thievish, untruthful, never right in opinions or judgment and inclined to swindle.

Jupiter in *Gemini* makes the body more plump but well-made and of middle height; graceful carriage. The complexion will not be clear; the eyes full, expressive, dark-grey or hazel; the hair brown; the behavior courteous, obliging and gentle; fond of the opposite sex and does well in responsible positions.

When Jupiter is adversely aspected in Gemini the person is shallow in intellect, stupid, silly, over-enthusiastic and very bad company; he is his own worst enemy.

Mars in *Gemini* denotes a tall, well-made, muscular body; fair complexion; blond or light brown hair; dark grey eyes with very good eyesight.

The disposition brave and confidant, bold, intellectual, quick-witted and deeply understanding; eloquent and inquisitive; a very active fancy.

When Mars is afflicted in Gemini the person will be intemperate, cruel, untruthful, inclined to evil deeds, will not stick to anything for long, and will be an imposter.

Sun in *Gemini* gives a well-made body of medium stature; good features and complexion; blond hair; light blue or brown eyes.

In disposition, intellectual, courteous, honorable, and possessed of many fine qualities. When afflicted, a cheater, a sceptic; unsettled, changeable, easy to impose upon, easy to influence and too sensitive to gain much success.

Venus or *Neptune* in *Gemini* describes a well-made, graceful body; full middle stature. The complexion is good and clear; lots of brown hair; hazel-grey eyes; beautiful hands with nicely shaped nails.

The disposition is charitable, honorable, liberal, gay and fond of social things, refined in taste and good in behavior. When evilly aspected, Venus in Gemini makes one very unconventional, dissipated, inconstant in affection, lustful, careless, mischievous, weak-minded and just a plain busy-body. Such persons make very bad husbands or wives.

Moon in *Gemini* describes a tall, well-made, beautiful body; very graceful in movement; good, clear complexion with lots of color; brown, curly hair.

The disposition is changeable but very agreeable, gentle, obliging, well-mannered and of refined mind. When the Moon is afflicted in Gemini the person is subtle, crafty, careless in person and of imprudent and destructive habits.

Cancer rising gives a short stature with the upper part of the body larger and better made than the lower; the carriage not good; the hands and feet short; large head and short neck; pale, clear complexion; small, dark eyes; dark or brown hair; full, well-shaped lips; pleasant voice. This is the *vital receptive* sign.

Moon in *Cancer* shows a medium stature, inclined to stoutness; an oval face; pale, dusky complexion; brown hair; blue eyes; full, well-shaped lips.

If the Moon is well aspected the pathway of life is brilliant; it strengthens the mind, gives mental energy, clever intellect, talent for many things. They "go places and do things" with ease and success, for they have strength of purpose.

When the Moon is badly aspected in Cancer they are wavering, lazy, addicted to bad habits, frivolous and uninteresting.

Sun in *Cancer* describes a small body, unhealthy in appearance; usually stout; a labored walk. Usually the hair is dark and the eyes are large, expressive, dark brown or hazel-grey.

In disposition, harmless, cheerful, fond of the opposite sex, finishes what they start but changeable, mediumistic, receptive; loves home and family, and possesses a retentive memory; fears ridicule, is industrious, conscientious, fruitful and productive.

When the *Sun* is afflicted in Cancer, usually obstinate, cruel, high-tempered, and desirous of "ruling the roost." This person will usually ruin his health through all kinds of dissipation because of an intense desire for change and excitement and intense emotion.

Uranus in *Cancer* describes one of short stature with broad shoulders; features are sharp and thin, nose slightly hooked, eyes small and restless; hair dark brown or black; dull complexion.

In disposition, the individual is studious with marked interest in the occult, of good mathematical ability and philosophic inclination; excellent mentality.

When Uranus is afflicted in Cancer the person is prone to acts of violence and injustice, is a mischief-maker, and possesses generally an evil disposition.

Saturn in *Cancer* gives medium height; thin, ill-made body; thin face with pale, sallow complexion; brown hair and dark eyes.

In disposition, profound in opinions, labors long and earnestly for accomplishment and gains much by earnest, patient study; a deep thinker.

When Saturn is badly aspected in Cancer the person is jealous, malicious, bigoted, superstitious, cowardly, envious, fearful and miserly.

Jupiter in *Cancer* describes a person of middle stature, inclined to a fleshy but well-made body; oval face; dark brown, curly hair; large, expressive hazel or brown eyes. Sometimes these people are broad-shouldered and massive.

In disposition, honorable, pious, self-sacrificing, compassionate, fortunate and fond of learning.

When badly aspected they are meddlers and busy-bodies, conceited and, if a man, will be a favorite among women; arrogant, indifferent, full of false pride, bigoted, weak and careless.

Mars in *Cancer* describes a short, wiry, muscular body with an active walk; dull complexion; thick, light brown or flaxen hair; sharp, hazel-grey eyes; hooked nose.

In disposition this person is generous, brave, stern, witty, crafty, ingenious and eloquent. Mars badly aspected gives cruelty, violence, revenge, addiction to drink; an imposter; gets all he can and gives little in return.

Venus or *Neptune* in *Cancer* is a short body, sometimes fleshy, or very thin; oval face, nice clear skin, and eyes either of an azure tint, dark hazel or even black; sweet voice; brown hair with perhaps a red tinge. Venus or Neptune in Cancer gives refinement, culture, sweet nature, modesty, and an aesthetic temperament.

When afflicted the person will be inconstant, lazy, not to be relied upon, interested in personal emotions.

Mercury in *Cancer* describes low stature; dull complexion; small, sharp-sighted eyes; thin face; sharp nose with wide nostrils; dull blond or brown hair; thin lips.

In disposition this person is clever, poetical, benevolent, mysterious, and possesses a strong memory. When Mercury in Cancer is better aspected than the Moon, ruler of the sign, the reasoning faculties will be better and stronger than the sensitive faculties.

When Mercury is evilly aspected in Cancer the person is changeable, worrying, imprudent and destructive; possesses wit but applies it to an evil purpose.

Leo rising gives the strongest and best formed body of all the signs with the exception of Libra. Leo is physically the strongest sign of the zodiac. It gives broad shoulders; broad, sometimes fat, face but a face with a very pleasant expression; commanding eyes; usually light, wavy hair; firm mouth; high forehead; and a good complexion.

The disposition is resolute, unbending, ambitious, and fixed in opinions. There is an over-abundance of Life Force. This is a *motive* sign.

Sun in *Leo* gives a strong, well-made body; regular features; fine, soft skin with lots of color; hair light brown or red-gold; full, prominent, golden-brown eyes; eyelashes and eyebrows darker than the hair.

The disposition is just, honorable, faithful, ambitious and much respected. When the Sun in Leo is badly aspected the person is restless and cruel, fond of ease and pleasure and a spendthrift.

Uranus in *Leo* describes one of upright carriage; broad shoulders; good complexion; strong bones; brown or auburn hair; full, dark eyes; Roman nose.

The disposition is inquisitive, ingenious and learned. When badly aspected, Uranus in Leo makes one eccentric, secretive and difficult to please.

Saturn in *Leo* describes a person of large bony structure with broad shoulders, wide chest and a long back; sometimes stooped; light hair and pale complexion.

The disposition is generous, passionate, of good mind but rather severe. Saturn in Leo adversely aspected denotes a coward when put to the test and one who never changes his opinions and who therefore stays in a rut.

Jupiter in *Leo* gives a strong, tall, well-made body; curly, light brown or blond hair; ruddy complexion; full, smiling, blue eyes; a very good looking person.

The disposition is courageous, magnanimous, masterful and the person will scorn all sordid actions. When under adverse aspects Jupiter in Leo produces a person who delights in arguments, one who is proud, vain, greedy, and selfish. "They rule or else."

Mars in *Leo* describes a well-made, wiry, muscular body; dark complexion; large, piercing eyes, probably light blue; lots of coarse, wiry hair; generous mouth; quick smile.

In disposition this person is cooperative, a good mixer, free-spirited and noble. Mars in Leo badly aspected makes one boastful, fond of pleasure and a lover of debate. He takes what he wants without permission.

Venus or *Neptune* in *Leo* describes a tall, beautifully made body; oval face; clear complexion; full, wide-open, light blue or brown eyes; flaxen or red hair. There may be a few freckles on the face.

The disposition is generous and proud, moderately faithful and good humored. When Venus is badly aspected the person is generous in the affections, too easily and quickly angered, and possesses no depth to the character.

Mercury in *Leo* describes a large body of medium height; swarthy or dull complexion; high, broad forehead; full, hazel-grey or brown eyes; a high nose; lots of light brown or blond hair.

In disposition this individual will be intellectually alert and keen, ambitious of honor, possessing a subtle political brain, and of great pride. If Mercury is badly aspected the person will be hasty, conceited and will not persevere.

Moon in *Leo* gives a tall, strong body with large bones, possibly quite fleshy; round face with a pleasant expression; good, clear complexion; light brown or blond hair; large, blue or blue-grey eyes.

In disposition the person is high-minded, proud, peaceable and generally fortunate. When the Moon is adversely aspected in Leo the person is over-sensitive and desirous of ruling; too free with the affections, over-indulgent in pleasure, venturesome, self-centered and of poor memory.

Virgo rising gives a person of average height or above, with a well-made, neat form; usually broad shoulders; an active walk; lots of dark brown hair; high broad forehead; dark eyes with a frank expression; straight, well-formed nose with wide, sensitive nostrils; small mouth with full lips; dusky complexion. This is the *mental* type.

The disposition is industrious, speculative, prudent, careful in details; good mental abilities.

Mercury in *Virgo* describes a tall, slender and well-proportioned body; sharp features; oval face and bad complexion; expressive, dark hazel eyes; long nose with sensitive nostrils; dark hair, perhaps black.

The disposition is ingenious and accomplished, speculative, intellectual, and skilled in physical science.

When Mercury is adversely aspected in Virgo, especially when retrograde, the person is skeptical, unsettled, changeable, vague, morose, of wavering mind and has many dishonorable qualities.

Uranus in *Virgo* describes a medium or tall, well-proportioned body; broad forehead; oval face; dark complexion; brown eyes which seem to have flecks or spots in them; straight, well-shaped nose; chestnut brown or black hair.

The disposition is clever, learned, very abrupt in manner, original, and independent; gain will come through public occupations.

Uranus in Virgo, badly aspected, gives lots of disappointment and difficulty, as well as strange and sudden bodily afflictions. It makes the person stubborn, wayward and eccentric.

Saturn in *Virgo* describes a tall or medium tall, thin body; high forehead; swarthy, perhaps sallow, complexion; long features; black or dark brown eyes and hair.

The disposition is reserved, subtle, studious, curious, discreet, and over-cautious. Under bad aspect, Saturn in Virgo makes one vindictive, malicious, treacherous, thievish and liable to mental diseases.

Jupiter in *Virgo* describes one of medium stature with a full sized, well-made body; a handsome person; dark, wavy hair; frank, red-brown eyes; large, well-shaped nose; ruddy but not clear complexion; well-shaped mouth; good teeth and a pleasant smile.

The disposition is materialistic, discreet, and prudent. The individual possesses wisdom, knowledge, honesty, and may gain through literature. When Jupiter in Virgo is badly aspected the person lacks concentration, is covetous, rash, critical, speculative, a boaster and mischief-maker.

Mars in *Virgo* describes a well-proportioned muscular body of medium height; dark brown or red-brown hair; broad, high-forehead; high cheek bones; large nose with wide nostrils; brown eyes; thin lips.

In disposition this person will be active, quick-witted, shrewd, tactful, discriminative, self-willed, forceful and energetic. Adversely aspected, Mars in Virgo gives a dishonest, irritable, overly critical person; one who is obstinate, proud, bad-tempered and revengeful.

Venus or *Neptune* in *Virgo* describes a medium or tall, well-proportioned body; a very good looking person. The hair will be flaxen or brown; expressive, hazel-grey or brown eyes; mouth and nose well-shaped; nice smile and perhaps dimples. This person will be a very neat dresser.

In disposition the person with Venus in Virgo will be of a quiet, even temper, ingenious mind, and deep, sincere feelings.

When Venus is afflicted in Virgo the person becomes vain, selfish, secretive, and unconventional. This is an unfortunate place for an afflicted Venus because the person lives a double life.

Moon in *Virgo* describes one of medium stature with an oval face, broad forehead, straight nose with rounded nostrils, well-shaped lips and pointed chin, chestnut-brown hair.

The disposition is very reserved, peaceable, trustworthy, talented and ambitious. The individual possesses a good memory and literary abilities. Under bad aspects Moon in Virgo makes one melancholy, boastful, tale-bearing, covetous, overly critical, and extremely unfortunate in relations with the opposite sex.

Sun in *Virgo* gives a tall, slender, well-proportioned body; good complexion; lots of dark brown hair; brown or blue-grey eyes.

In disposition the person is extremely ambitious, confident, rather cheerful, modest, a lover of order and beauty, a good reasoner. When the Sun is afflicted in Virgo the person is quick-tempered, fearful, discontented, and holds malice.

Libra rising describes a tall, well-formed, finely built body; long head; small, regular features; usually has dimples; good teeth; well-formed nose, mouth and chin; hair usually very fine and light in color. This is the *motive vital* temperament.

The person born with Libra rising is a lover of justice and must have peace and harmony. Courteousness, kindness, agreeableness, generosity, intuition, inspiration and a good mentality belong to this sign.

Sun in *Libra* gives a tall, upright, well-made body; a very fine looking person. The hair is light brown or blond; full, blue-grey or brown, very expressive eyes; ruddy complexion, and sometimes there is a rash or pimples on the face.

The disposition is courteous and pleasant. These people are natural peace-makers. They usually marry young and more than once. This is the great lover in either sex.

When badly aspected the Sun in Libra makes a weak character, a very changeable, untruthful, selfish and self-indulgent person who depends too much on other people and is changeable and dual in nature.

Venus or *Neptune* in *Libra* describes a tall, beautiful body with a small waist; clear skin; oval face; dimples; very fine, brown hair; well-rounded, blue or soft brown eyes; sweet voice a kind expression.

The disposition will be refined, cheerful, happy, charitable, modest, and fond of the arts and sciences. When Venus is adversely aspected the person is lustful, timid, careless, lazy, self-indulgent, vulgar, shameless, and lacks discrimination.

Uranus in *Libra* describes a tall and a good-looking though sometimes stout body. The complexion will be good with some color in it; smooth brown hair; grey or hazel-grey eyes; high forehead.

In disposition this person is faithful, trustworthy and independent; an accomplished, intellectual mind and keen foresight. Afflicted, Uranus in Libra makes one overly forceful, abrupt, willful, unconventional, and very eccentric; much trouble through the opposite sex.

Saturn in *Libra* describes a well-made body with rather large bones; medium stature; usually good looking with a clear complexion, brown hair, dark blue or brown eyes, oval face and large nose.

In disposition the person is fond of debate, intellectual, fond of science and of refined tastes. Saturn in Libra adversely aspected creates a narrow-minded, opinionated person who must be boss, who loves to argue but who side-steps the issues and will not or cannot see the other fellow's side of the question; crafty; jealous; suspicious and vengeful.

Jupiter in *Libra* describes a tall, slender and well-proportioned body; chestnut brown hair; kindly blue or blue-grey eyes; well-formed nose which is inclined to be full at the tip; well-shaped mouth; good teeth; nice smile and dimples in the chin; also a clear, fresh complexion, sometimes freckled.

The disposition is kind, thoughtful, generous, much respected and admired by all, very obliging, industrious and friendly; usually honorable marriage. Jupiter adversely aspected in Libra makes one vain, greedy, over-boastful and always anxious to receive recognition.

Mars in *Libra* describes a well-proportioned, wiry body of medium height; light or soft brown hair; bright blue eyes; small mouth with full lips; short, Grecian nose. This person will be fond of the opposite sex, confident of his ability, cheerful, overly generous.

When badly aspected, Mars in Libra indicates one who is cruel, unconventional, addicted to bad habits, extravagant and loving luxury.

Mercury in *Libra* gives a tall, beautifully made body; a fine looking person; clear complexion with a good bit of color in it; an oval face with a broad forehead; well-shaped nose, mouth and chin; luxurious, soft, light brown hair.

The disposition is intellectual, virtuous, quite prudent, clever, and accurate in judgment. Mercury badly aspected in Libra makes one scatter-brained, easily hurt, covetous, deceitful, of bad judgment and petty in small things; untruthful.

Moon in *Libra* gives a tall, well-made body; beautiful complexion; lots of color; light brown or blond hair; eyelashes and eyebrows darker than the hair; large, azure blue or deep violet eyes.

In disposition this individual is changeable but pleasing, popular, good-natured, romantic, skilled in arts and crafts. The Moon afflicted in Libra makes one dishonorable, unconventional, brooding, treacherous, lazy, untidy, secretive, changeable, and mean.

Scorpio rising describes a person of average height or slightly below; strong, well-made body and a tendency to stoutness; thick, dark brown or red-brown, curly or wavy hair; blue or green-grey eyes; large nose; broad, round forehead; forceful chin; firm mouth lower lip fuller than the upper; a dimple in the cheek or chin. This is *motive vital* temperament.

Sun in *Scorpio* describes a square build full, fleshy body; broad shoulders; full broad forehead; dull complexion; light brown hair; blue-grey or brown, deep-set eyes; large nose, firm chin.

The disposition is determined, shrewd, keen, ambitious, quick-witted, courageous, strong willed and strong characteristics. The Sun in Scorpio adversely aspected makes one sarcastic, resentful, destructive, and of mean disposition.

Mars in *Scorpio* gives a strong, well-made body; medium stature; swarthy complexion; dark or auburn, curly or wiry hair; dark brown, keen, deep-set eyes that see every detail; a Roman nose; firm mouth and chin; broad, full forehead.

In disposition the person will be sharp, keen, diplomatic, firm, positive, determined in mind and will gain much knowledge. Mars badly aspected in Scorpio indicates one of bad temper, passionate, vengeful, ungrateful, overbearing, skeptical, and regarding no person's rights but his own.

Uranus in *Scorpio* gives a short, well-made body with broad, thick shoulders; rather long face; broad forehead; large nose; dark hair; dark eyes with a snappy expression; dark complexion.

In disposition the person with Uranus in Scorpio will have great determination and will power, persistence and a spirit that will not be broken by resistance or obstacles; an intuitive and inventive, conscientious, reserved, thoughtful person with firm and retentive memory.

Uranus adversely aspected in Scorpio makes one eccentric, malicious, impulsive, revolutionary, self-willed, abrupt, critical and dangerous.

Saturn in *Scorpio* describes a thick, ill-made body with broad shoulders; middle stature; a strong constitution; swarthy complexion; thick, dark hair; dark eyes; long, hooked nose; thin lips.

The disposition is resourceful, cautious, persistent, profoundly intellectual, of shrewd mind, and independent. Saturn afflicted in Scorpio gives a surly disposition; one who retains malice and anger, never admits defeat or that he is wrong; jealous, crafty, miserly and cruel.

Jupiter in *Scorpio* describes a person of middle stature with a stout, compact body; brown hair; full, brown eyes; a Roman nose; large mouth and firm chin.

In disposition a deeply emotional nature, powerful will, great ambition and stability of purpose. Jupiter adversely aspected causes the person to be extremely selfish and possessive, overindulgent with the opposite sex, of quick sarcastic temper and very jealous.

Venus or *Neptune* in *Scorpio* describes a middle stature; stout and well-made body; broad face; dark, curly hair; dusky complexion; dark blue or deep brown eyes; straight nose with round nostrils; dimple in the cheek or chin.

In disposition very generous, affectionate, lavish, loves ease and pleasure. Venus and Neptune are not well placed in Scorpio unless well aspected; under adverse aspect they make one guilty of many vicious actions.

Mercury in *Scorpio* describes a well-made body of medium stature; broad shoulders; curly brown hair; blue-grey or green eyes; swarthy complexion; short nose with an up-turned broad tip; well-shaped mouth and chin.

The disposition is subtle, studious, careful of its own interests, clear and ingenious mind. When Mercury is adversely aspected in Scorpio the person will be crafty, deceitful, obstinate, reckless, and fond of the opposite sex.

Moon in *Scorpio* describes a short, thick, heavy-set person with dark, brown or black hair; dark eyes; pale, sallow skin; small mouth with full lips.

The disposition is self-confident, determined, independent, self-sustaining. The Moon adversely aspected in Scorpio indicates one who is abrupt, aggressive, quick-tempered, self-indulgent, treacherous, malicious, and very unfaithful.

Sagittarius rising gives a strong, well-formed, wiry body which is usually over medium height and inclined to stoop a little. The face is oval or long; high, broad forehead; dark-hazel or blue-grey, wide-open, expressive eyes; clear complexion; long, well-shaped nose with round sensitive nostrils; well-shaped mouth and chin; brown or chestnut colored hair that grows back from the temples and inclines to baldness. This is a *mental motive* temperament.

Jupiter in *Sagittarius* gives a tall, upright, well-formed, muscular body; an oval face of fine expression; wide-open, hazel-grey or dark brown eyes; thick, chestnut brown or dark brown hair.

The disposition is obliging, noble, free-spirited, industrious, friendly, generous, tolerant, optimistic, philosophical and generally successful. Under evil aspect the person will be bigoted, timid, arrogant, careless and indifferent.

Sun in *Sagittarius* describes a tall, upright, well-made body with broad shoulders; auburn or light brown hair, probably wavy; broad features; color in the complexion; large, expressive, wide-open eyes that are light grey, or green-grey in color; small mouth with well-formed lips.

In disposition the person is frank, outspoken, truthful to a fault, sometimes overly blunt, not easily discouraged, of strong will when interested, energetic, usually prophetic and knows the next move before you do, loves liberty and freedom.

Under adverse aspect the Sun in Sagittarius produces a person who is debased, obstinate, lacking in principle, unwilling to admit defeat; usually lives at another's expense and expects to gain even if it is at another's loss. Many times he is cruel and ill-tempered.

Uranus in *Sagittarius* denotes a tall, full-sized, graceful body with strong bones; clear complexion; thin face with prominent features; dark eyes and hair.

The disposition is hasty but careful, extremely proud, fond of money and sports, of unlimited imagination and broad, intellectual mind, progressive, daring, adventuresome, intuitive, and a sincere friend.

Adversely aspected Uranus in Sagittarius shows a hypocrite who does not "practice what he preaches"; deceitful, regretful, fatalistic, of unsteady mind, easily unbalanced, extremely sensitive and nervous.

Saturn in *Sagittarius* gives a large, raw-boned person who is thin and of good, though pale, complexion. The forehead is high and the eyebrows close to the nose which is long and sometimes hooked; the hair and eyes are usually dark.

In disposition this person is careful, obliging, a good friend, merciful to an enemy, profound in religion and opinions, and the original hater of crime. Saturn adversely aspected in Sagittarius makes one fretful, envious, very bigoted, prejudiced, promises things that cannot be fulfilled.

Mars in *Sagittarius* denotes a tall, muscular, well-made, wiry body; an oval face; brown hair with a possible auburn tinge to it; good complexion; good features; small, well-shaped mouth; quick, penetrating, brown or blue-grey eyes.

The disposition is cheerful, active, courteous, generous, brave, ambitious, intellectual and impulsive, fond of argument but good natured about it, very original.

Under bad aspect, Mars in Sagittarius makes a person overly venturesome, tricky, overly fond of pleasure, inclined to exaggerate, skeptical, unorthodox in ideas and beliefs, usually a religious bigot. They have many dual experiences.

Venus or *Neptune* in *Sagittarius* describes a tall handsome, graceful, well-proportioned body; nice clear skin of good color; light or brown wavy hair; light blue or soft brown, expressive eyes; oval face; short nose with round, sensitive nostrils; dimples in the cheeks or chin; nice smile.

In disposition this person is obliging, refined, impressionable, intuitive, imaginative, creative, romantic, religious, a lover of beauty in all forms and much attracted to the opposite sex.

Under adverse aspect Venus in Sagittarius makes one fickle, passionate, bad tempered, self-indulgent and selfish, overly sensitive, emotional, vague and indefinite.

Mercury in *Sagittarius* describes a tall, well-formed, slender, large-boned body; ruddy complexion; plenty of light brown hair; expressive, green-grey or blue-grey eyes; large features; long nose with sensitive nostrils; long, flexible, well-shaped lips; long hands and fingers.

The disposition is ambitious, independent, impulsive, active mentally and physically, interested in religion and philosophy, science and law.

When Mercury is badly aspected in Sagittarius the person is rash, impulsive, often rebellious, lacking in judgment, very changeable, too dual in nature.

Moon in *Sagittarius* gives a good-looking person of medium height; oval face; good complexion; brown hair; blue or dark grey eyes; nice features.

In disposition the individual is very honorable, gains respect, is ambitious, kind-hearted, sociable, loves religion and philosophy and is correct in customs and judgment.

Moon adversely aspected, the person is restless, unsettled, addicted to bad habits, overly sensitive, and inclined to make promises with no intention of keeping them.

Capricorn rising gives medium stature, usually slender, sometimes of thin, bony structure; long features; prominent, thin neck; sharp chin; dark brown or black hair. This is the *vital mental* temperament.

Saturn in *Capricorn* describes a lean, raw-boned body; medium stature; one who walks with a stride; dull brown or black hair; blue or dark brown eyes; thin face and a dull, sallow complexion.

The disposition is grave, serious, cautious, ambitious, and persistent. The individual is a good reasoner and a deep thinker.

Saturn adversely aspected in Capricorn makes one discontented, peevish, covetous, suspicious, unforgiving, fatalistic, discontented, stubborn, resentful, and inclined to retain anger.

Sun in *Capricorn* gives medium height; an angular body; high forehead; long nose; thin lips; strong, narrow chin; piercing blue or dark brown eyes.

The disposition is thoughtful, serious, dignified, careful, cautious, and persistent. He has a deep mind, much self-esteem, is never discouraged but often disappointed, and makes the most of every opportunity.

The Sun afflicted in Capricorn gives a bad temper, hasty judgment, selfishness, self-centeredness. This person will seize every circumstance to better himself.

Uranus in *Capricorn* gives medium stature; lean, wiry body and a quick, active walk; high forehead; thin features; small, dark and piercing eyes.

The disposition is reserved, secretive, extremely ambitious, very independent, dependable, and deeply thoughtful.

Adversely aspected Uranus in Capricorn gives bad-temper, eccentricity, radicalism, stubbornness, jealousy, and a critical mind. They are subject to reversals and separations.

Jupiter in *Capricorn* describes one of middle height and adds weight to the body; broad shoulders; pale complexion, possibly freckled; large nose; thin face; dark brown hair.

The disposition is serious and deliberate, constructive, ambitious to gain recognition, which is usually achieved, and organizational ability.

Jupiter afflicted in Capricorn gives a miserly, stingy, lazy, complaining, envious, critical, self-centered person. He always believes every one to be wrong but himself and sees that he gets what he wants at the other person's expense.

Mars in *Capricorn* describes a lean, muscular body; small stature; small head; sharp features; thin, dark hair; dark, pale complexion with probable blemishes or freckles; grey or light blue, deep-set eyes.

In disposition the person is witty, shrewd, penetrating, courageous, self-reliant, ambitious, industrious, successful in all undertakings and responsible; gains much through the intuition.

Mars adversely aspected in Capricorn makes the person irritable, quick-tempered, very passionate, too aggressive, not too honest, has much difficulty over affairs in general and much conflict.

Venus or *Neptune* in *Capricorn* gives average height; pale complexion; sad brown or dark hair; blue or brown eyes.

In disposition the person is fond of pleasure, ambitious, diplomatic, careful of honor, respectable. Badly aspected Venus in Capricorn gives a social snob and a person who is cold, calculating, treacherous, unfortunate and subject to sudden changes and strange catastrophes.

Mercury in *Capricorn* describes a medium stature; crooked legs; thin face with sharp features; upturned nose or a nose that is sharp at the tip; dusky complexion; brown or blond hair.

The disposition is active, sharp, penetrating, diplomatic, careful, serious, economical, and practical, possessing organizing ability. Mercury badly aspected, the person will be peevish, calculating, covetous, fickle, discontented, extremely restless, speculative; a busy-body and tale-bearer.

Moon in *Capricorn* describes a thin, small, weak body; low stature; thin face and features; pale, sallow complexion; bright blue or slate-grey eyes; brown hair; ill-shaped legs or weak knees.

The disposition is cautious, honorable, ambitious; inspires confidence. The person is a good organizer. Adversely aspected *Moon* in Capricorn gives a person who makes enemies easily, who is lax in the control of the appetites, weak in character, calculating, cold, unfeeling. "Just plain ornery."

Aquarius rising gives a well-formed person of medium height with a robust, healthy, strong body; good, clear complexion; attractive features; broad forehead; expressive, wide-set, grey, blue or hazel eyes. A very handsome person. This is a *mental motive* temperament.

Uranus in *Aquarius* describes a full-built, well-made body of medium height; good-sized and well-shaped head; broad, low forehead, prominent at the temples; clear, fresh complexion; straight nose, rounded at the tip; hazel eyes; brown, wavy hair.

These individuals are faithful, truthful, sincere, patient, industrious, original, and of good mentality, strong imagination and intuition; pleasant, sociable and obliging.

Adversely aspected the person with Uranus in Aquarius will be eccentric, peculiar, unconventional, unmannerly, temperamental, unforgiving. He will be characterized by all sorts of peculiar mannerisms. It is impossible to control this person because he prefers to be bad.

Sun in *Aquarius* gives middle stature; well-made, rather large body; round, full face; broad, low forehead; good, clear complexion; wide-apart, expressive, hazel-grey eyes; attractive mouth and chin; light brown hair; usually very good-looking.

The disposition is quiet, determined, faithful, refined, generous, cautious, steady, intelligent, studious, thoughtful, possessed of good reasoning faculties.

The Sun afflicted in Aquarius makes a person radical, changeable, stubborn, resentful, temperamental, worrying; not very profound; a cruel boss.

Saturn in *Aquarius* describes a large-boned, strong body of medium height which sometimes is very stout; large head and face; broad, high forehead, prominent at the temples; long nose; thin but well-shaped lips; clear complexion; brown hair deep blue or dark brown eyes.

In disposition this person is profound in wit, good in all the arts and sciences, thoughtful, reserved, serious, of penetrating intellect, very impressive when interested; a deep thinker; makes many acquaintances.

Adversely aspected Saturn in Aquarius makes one crafty, jealous, suspicious, subtle, mistrustful, melancholy, selfish and self-interested.

Jupiter in *Aquarius* describes a medium stature; large, well-made body; brown hair, perhaps tinged with red or red-gold; clear, fresh complexion with lots of color in it; red-brown or deep-blue eyes which are large and smiling; eyelashes and eyebrows darker than the hair; well-shaped nose, inclined to be fleshy at the end; firm, rather prominent chin.

The disposition is faithful, sincere, just, merciful, obliging, original, and even tempered; a broad, liberal mind. Adversely aspected Jupiter in Aquarius creates a hypocrite—one who is conceited, vain, indifferent, and greedy.

Mars in *Aquarius* gives a rather tall, muscular body; sandy or red hair; fair complexion; light blue or grey eyes; well-shaped features.

In disposition the person is very original and convincing, intellectual, independent, fond of science, fixed in opinions; possesses much vitality and mental energy.

Under bad aspect, Mars in Aquarius makes a person very abrupt, blunt, reckless, rude, ill-mannered with vulgar, coarse ways. The individual cannot be depended upon in an emergency and makes a false friend.

Venus or *Neptune* in *Aquarius* describes a handsome person of medium height with a beautifully made body; graceful carriage; good, clear complexion; wide-set, expressive, hazel-grey or green-grey eyes; light brown or blond, soft, curly hair; broad, low forehead; long sweeping brows and long eyelashes; upturned nose; nicely shaped mouth and chin with dimples; a pleasant voice. Eye color is changeable.

If these planets are in good aspect to Jupiter the person will be handsome or beautiful. In disposition the person is cheerful, philosophic, friendly, generous, intuitive, reserved in opinion, sincere in conviction, popular, fond of the opposite sex and the arts and sciences. Venus afflicted in Aquarius makes one passionate, jealous, sensual, addicted to bad habits and depraved tastes.

Mercury in *Aquarius* denotes middle stature; a body that is inclined to be fleshy; full face; clear complexion; brown hair; blue-grey eyes; very intelligent expression.

The disposition is obliging and charitable, witty, refined, original. The person is a keen judge of human nature, a good reasoner and deep thinker. Mercury badly aspected in Aquarius makes the person restless, boastful, quarrelsome, sarcastic, envious, untruthful, scheming.

Moon in *Aquarius* describes middle stature; a large, well-formed body; clear, pale complexion; large, deep blue or red-brown eyes with a restless expression; dark hair.

The disposition is agreeable, friendly, courteous, sympathetic, independent, very original, and of good reasoning faculties.

The Moon afflicted in Aquarius makes one unconventional, eccentric, overly sensitive and secretive with Bohemian tendencies.

Pisces rising usually denotes a person of short stature, though such is not always the case. Sometimes the Piscean is of middle stature and inclined to be stout. The body is ill-made, poorly shaped or weak. The complexion is delicate, pale and clear; the forehead, broad, low and full at the temples; shapely head; hazel or grey eyes; well-shaped and good-looking lips. This is the *vital motive* temperament.

Neptune or *Venus* in *Pisces* gives middle stature; a body that is inclined to be fleshy but well-made; clear skin and good complexion; dimples in the cheek or chin; short nose, round or up-tilted at the tip; brown, curly hair; wide-apart, expressive, changeable, blue-grey, blue-green or hazel eyes; brows darker than the hair and well-marked.

The disposition is mild, just, peaceful, compassionate, sensitive, psychic, emotional and inspirational, broad-minded, easily moved to sympathy and of profound thought.

Under adverse aspect, Neptune or Venus in Pisces makes one suffer through the emotions and sympathies, love peace, be unscrupulous, addicted to bad habits, lazy, emotionally unsound.

Sun in *Pisces* denotes one of medium height with a body that fluctuates in weight though it is usually fleshy; round face; good complexion; well-shaped mouth and chin, but sometimes a double-chin; brown or flaxen hair which is curly and thick; large, wide-apart, expressive, blue-grey or hazel eyes.

In disposition this person will possess a kind and loving nature, be honest, sympathetic, neat, particular, industrious but changeable, imaginative, inspirational; gifted with mediumistic faculties; fond of the unusual, secret, occult or psychic investigations; and logical in conclusions.

The Sun afflicted in Pisces makes one too much addicted to self-gratification, deprives one of self-confidence, creates selfishness and self-indulgence.

Jupiter in *Pisces* indicates one of medium stature with a fleshy, broad-shouldered body; dull complexion; brown or flaxen hair; blue or deep brown eyes that are very expressive and wide-apart as well as large.

The disposition is intuitive, studious, sociable, quiet, unassuming, sympathetic, liberal, generous and of broad views.

Afflicted Jupiter in Pisces makes the individual changeable, too fond of pleasure, indolent, dull, stupid, deceitful, idle, worthless, and easily influenced; does not make a good husband or wife.

Uranus in *Pisces* describes one of medium height with a large, well-made body; pale complexion; oval face with a high broad forehead; dark brown hair; expressive, dark, grey eyes.

In disposition the person is just, proud, fond of debate, fond of occult investigation and research. Adversely aspected Uranus in Pisces gives a peculiar nature; a malicious mind and mean conduct; a very critical person, adventuresome and will have many strange experiences.

Saturn in *Pisces* describes middle stature; a good-sized body; large head and face; pale, sallow complexion; full, dark eyes; dark hair; bad teeth; long nose drooping mouth; pointed chin.

The disposition is ingenious, aspiring, steady, persistent, practical, deep and intuitive.

Saturn adversely aspected in Pisces makes the person fickle and not to be trusted, cold and calculating, lacking in firmness and application. Circumstances very often decide things for him.

Mars in *Pisces* denotes a person of medium stature with a short, fleshy body; a bad complexion; sharp, shrewd, light blue or brown eyes; dark hair. This person is not good looking.

The disposition is generous, affectionate, apt in details, cautious; desirous of attainment and accomplishes much quietly.

Mars badly aspected in Pisces makes a person bold, depressed, gloomy, indolent, irresolute, untruthful, dishonest, ignorant and very unfortunate.

Mercury in *Pisces* describes a medium or rather tall person who is awkward but energetic; a broad, high forehead; deep-set, blue-grey or hazel-grey eyes; quick sight; straight nose, up-turned or fleshy at the tip; brown, curly hair; pale complexion.

The disposition is adaptable, sympathetic and understanding. This person will gain through study or by intuitive perception and will rarely be at a loss to explain things. He possesses numerous abilities, and is analytical, diplomatic, and good-natured.

Afflicted Mercury in Pisces makes one scatter-brained, addicted to bad habits, a braggart, especially about things about which they know nothing, and overly receptive; has too many "irons in the fire" and is not good at anything.

Moon in *Pisces* describes low stature; a plump body; pale complexion; brown, curly hair, though sometimes blond; large blue or blue-grey eyes with a soft expression; sometimes wears glasses as the eyes are weak or else has a squint to the eyes; short nose with round, flexible nostrils; well-shaped, full mouth.

The disposition is kind, quiet, retiring, very sensitive, inspirational, mediumistic; loves harmony and beauty, possesses keen perception and a powerful and fruitful imagination, and could be a successful speaker, writer or composer.

Under adverse aspect the Moon in Pisces makes a person lazy, misunderstood, inconstant, of bad habits, easily discouraged, meeting many obstacles; usually suffers through misunderstanding and has a hard time with self-expression.

Questions Relating to Each of the Twelve Houses and the Meaning of the Planets in the Houses

First House Questions

The first house answers questions concerning the health, circumstances, accidents, mind, form and stature of the querent; the state of a ship at sea; voyages; fathers of kings, the fourth from the tenth; wives of enemies, the seventh from the seventh; journeys of children, the ninth from the fifth; friends of brethren, the eleventh from the third; and the success of any enterprise.

Planets in the First House

Neptune in the first. Indecision concerning circumstances. If badly aspected or in its fall or detriment, will have a bad effect on health, devitalizing the nervous system. Usually an alias or change of name with Neptune here. When well aspected, especially to the Sun, Moon, Jupiter or Venus, brings vibration of great spiritual faith, high aspirations, and benefits to the career. Also gives an extremely uncommon personality, with an odd or strange point of view.

Badly aspected, and depending on the sign it is in, it ages a person; gives a stoop to the figure; makes a person either thin or ill-shaped with fat, sometimes with malformation.

Uranus in the first. Some strange, unexpected and vexatious occurrences are about to take place; unsettled in mind; interested in extraordinary and uncommon objects, especially such things as the house of which it is the ruler signifies. If well aspected the sudden action will be more advantageous.

If afflicted by the Moon or Venus, unhappiness in courtship and marriage. The querent loves to travel and is fond of novelty, romantic in his ideas, and fond of antique things.

Saturn in the first. Gives heavy thoughts about the matter in question; pain in the teeth when young, and probably loss of some front teeth. The querent will not be in good health; is subject to blows, bruises, falls, and given to shed tears. The disposition is thoughtful, reserved, fearful, firm in opinions and not easily moved.

Jupiter in the first. Unafflicted, denotes a good constitution. He is cheerful, sincere and much respected; acts honorably and is generally fortunate; success attends him.

Mars in the first. Is evil, subjects the querent to burns, scalds, cuts, scars or marks in the head or face; uneasiness of mind, quarrels, hot temper; is a liar, boaster; fond of disputation, and this according as Mars is dignified.

Sun in the first. Gives a degree of pride, and if in good aspect with the Moon, success in life, unless the Sun is in Libra or Aquarius; but if badly aspected, rash and injurious; makes the querent a boaster. If in aspect with Mars, the querent is involved in love affairs about the age of nineteen years.

In bad aspect of Uranus, Saturn or Mars, then bad health and danger of accidents; if well aspected, long life and good health; fond of public employments. Sun's evil aspect denotes death of relatives; disgrace; loss of friends and honor.

Venus in the first. Free from affliction, good fortune; lives honorably; has quiet, mild disposition, though given to pleasure, which will be detrimental to the health. Venus well aspected, gain by means of females.

If afflicted by Mars, the querent is unconventional; if by Saturn, a fraud. Venus ascending gives strength to the constitution, yet makes one too fond of following after the animal inclinations; if in her debility, inclined to be immoral.

Mercury in the first. If well dignified, the querent is a good speaker; is restless, fond of traveling; has a busy, active mind. But if afflicted or retrograde, then a short memory and frequent disappointments, with a bad delivery; very skeptical; or has no ability to speak in public.

Mercury square the Moon, great disappointments; is slandered and has sorrow from that house from which the aspect is thrown, and of those houses of which these planets are the rulers. If close to the Sun, the mind will be profound.

Moon in the first. Fond of traveling. If afflicting the malefics, then bad health, uneasiness of mind and trouble according to the house it governs; given to drinking, sensuousness, low morals. If strong and well aspected, healthful.

If afflicted by the Sun, liable to injuries to the eyes; in good aspect to the Sun, marries respectably. In whatever sign the Moon is, will denote a mole or mark on that part of the body.

Part of Fortune in the first. Riches—and the person makes his own fortune, especially if in good aspect to Venus, Jupiter, the Sun or Moon.

Moon's Nodes in the first. The North Node gives honesty; the South Node dishonesty, and the querent will attempt to deceive you and will not deal fairly; therefore beware of him. He is in great anxiety of mind, and will very likely be pock-marked or otherwise blemished in the face.

The *ruler* of the *first*. In its fall or detriment, the querent despairs of the matter. Very likely has only one parent alive. Conjunct the South Node, injury to the character and health, and other damage according to the house in which it is placed.

Second House Questions

All questions concerning money; wealth or poverty; loaned money; loss or gain in movable things; money that is used in speculation or law suits or whatever the seventh house shows;

denotes our possessions; trade of children, being the tenth from the fifth; private enemies of brethren or of our first brother or sister, being the twelfth from the third.

It is the death of the wife or husband, partners or sweethearts, and public enemies, being the eighth from the seventh.

Planets in the Second House

Neptune in the second, danger of being drawn into bogus monetary dealings. If badly aspected, the person will be on the receiving end, and will not care to earn his own money.

Neptune here in good aspect, money gained through some uncommon means—could be through large animals, stock, etc.

Uranus in the second, many changes and unsettled money matters. *Uranus*, *Saturn*, or *Mars* here strong and well aspected, denote that the querent's substance will change from bad to good. The *Moon* unafflicted gives money; afflicted, the reverse. The *Sun*, *Mars* or the *Dragon's Tail* in this house signifies a perpetual waste, with sometimes poverty. *Jupiter* or the *Part of Fortune* here denotes success in money matters, if not afflicted. *Venus* gives money, according to her dignities or debilities; Venus, wherever she is, gives the love of the things of that house. *Mercury* gives loss or gain (according to its placement) by learning, books, etc.

The ruler of the second house afflicted or retrograde brings loss of money loaned, or a debt. Three or more planets here, great want of money; if they are badly aspected and in their detriment, much poverty.

Third House Questions

All questions concerning brethren, neighbors; short journeys; removals of manufacturers; our first brother or sister; blood relatives; rumors, reports, letters, messages; children of friends, being the fifth from the eleventh; sickness of kings or people in power, being the sixth from the tenth; friends of children, being the eleventh from the fifth; private enemies of the father or mother, being the twelfth from the fourth; children, churches, clerks, sects, dreams, mutations; long journeys of the lover, husband or wife, being the ninth from the seventh; honor and trade of servants, being the tenth from the sixth.

Planets in the Third House

Neptune in the third gives a highly imaginative and clairvoyant mind; a square or opposition of Venus and the Moon, strange journeys; deceit and fraud of relatives; with a square or opposition of the Moon and Mercury, hallucinations and madness; an evil mind; a good aspect to Jupiter here gives an inspired and spiritual imagination.

Uranus here brings frequent warnings; many disputes among relatives, neighbors, or so-called friends; well aspected, gain through journeys, and a clever mind. *Saturn* here is somewhat the same; also loss by journey, or inability to keep appointments; well aspected, a seeker of knowledge. *Jupiter*, success in short journeys, and a favorite with blood relatives, according to the planet's dignity. *Mars*, spiteful neighbors; quarrels with relatives; evil for journeys; some danger of being robbed; want of money. *Sun*, good comes from relatives and neighbors; much pleasure through kindred; love of travel. *Venus*, good for journeys; brethren, has pious neighbors; may marry a neighbor. *Mercury*, crafty relatives; swift journeys; learning accompanied by writing. *Moon* well aspected in cardinal signs, many short journeys for pleasure or health. If the Moon is afflicted, the parents suffer. *Dragon's Head*, good neighbors and relatives. *Dragon's Tail*, the reverse. *Part of Fortune*, gain through all third house affairs, especially writing or publishing, also by all fourth and fifth house affairs.

Fourth House Questions

Answers questions concerning the father or mother of the querent; land, houses, estates, entrenchments, castles; hidden things; things mislaid; gardens, orchards, and fields; the end of everything; dead men's goods; substance of the brethren, being the second from the third; children of private enemies, being the fifth from the twelfth; sickness of friends, being the sixth from the eleventh; it is the purchasing or renting of land; trade the husband, being the tenth from the seventh.

Planets in the Fourth House

Neptune in the fourth house in evil aspect to the Sun, Moon, or planets, danger of losing one's liberty; or poverty of environment; loneliness and depression. In good aspect to Mercury or Saturn, interest and help through occultism; to Venus, money and happiness by some unusual means. The bad aspects bring an element of trickery and fraud into the home life.

Uranus here, the person will have lost a parent; may lose property; and may inherit through friends. Great love for the father. If afflicted, parents do not live long. Many disputes about inheritance. *Saturn*, often annoyed about money matters connected with the right of the family; success at close of life. *Jupiter* here is more fortunate; probably a legacy will be left the native.

Peaceful home life. *Mars* here, the parents are either dead or in distress; gain through the dead; trouble over inheritance; person probably dissipates his inheritance or substance. The *Sun* here declares the father to be noble-minded; honor in old age; benefit through grandparents. *Venus* gives the same; may gain property through marriage. *Mercury*, gain by learning and the crafts. The *Moon* here, gain through parents. The querent owns property and if the *Part of Fortune* is here, he will improve it; gain through property and all fourth house affairs.

Fifth House Questions

Answers questions concerning children, pregnancy; personal substance of the father, being the second from the fourth; the success of messengers and ambassadors; pleasure; charters, lotteries, all games of chance, and speculation for pleasure; horse racing; betting; football; all games for recreation; bowling, tennis, baseball; dancing, music; death of those in official positions such as monarchs or presidents, being the eighth from the tenth; clubs, hills; mountain resorts; love affairs.

Planets in the Fifth House

Neptune in the fifth, illicit loves; fondness for dancing and the theater; great love of sensuous pleasure; secret love affairs; sorrows through love, speculation and children; gives intuition and sensitive foresight; accurate interpretation of human feelings. Badly aspected to the Moon, Venus or Mars, the feelings sway the reason; sickness through too lavish expenditure of emotional energy; too impulsive. Mysterious conditions arise through children and matters of affection; trouble and sickness through childbirth.

Uranus, Saturn, Mars or the *Dragon's Tail* here, unwanted children; only small family, and very disobedient offspring; great danger of miscarriage. *Jupiter* or *Venus* here gives good children; fortunate for speculation. The *Sun*, few children, but they will be high-minded and virtuous. *Mercury*, some annoyance from children; they may be sickly. Maybe illness through too much pleasure. *Moon* here in Pisces, Scorpio or Cancer, large family. *Part of Fortune*, gain through children and speculation, or whatever the fifth house promises.

If the *ruler* of the fifth cusp or planets in the fifth house are in bad aspect to the ruler of the eighth cusp, or planets in the eighth, there will be many sacrifices made in connection with all fifth and eighth house matters. A sacrifice will probably be made in an emotional matter or for a child.

Many planets in the fifth, the querent or person will be given to pleasure, or lives dishonorably with someone, or may live at a public place in some resort. A planet in the fifth *exalted*, the person may be talented in dancing, and will be fond of amusements of all kinds. *Venus, ruler* of the fifth, in Cancer in the eighth denotes the querent's (if a woman) first child will be a girl; that she will have chiefly female children; and that some of them may die.

The eighth house is fourth from the fifth, and is the end of fifth house affairs. If the planets ruling the cusps of these houses are afflicting each other, the affairs ruled by these two houses will not have a happy ending.

Sixth House Questions

Questions concerning servants; small cattle and animals; the recovery of a sick person; the cause of disease and sickness and whether of long or short duration; particulars relating to aunts and uncles, being the third from the fourth; stewards; tenants; shepherds; farmers; substance of children, especially our first child, being the second from the fifth; death of a friend, being the eighth from the eleventh; long journeys of persons in power, being the ninth from the tenth; private enemies of wives and husbands or our intimate associates, being the twelfth from the seventh; and to some extent those connected with the army and navy.

Planets in the Sixth House

Neptune in the sixth, very little personal comfort; trouble with small animals, and loss of some; trouble through employers; limitation on account of sickness; consumption, or wasting disease.

Uranus here, indisposition of body; family sickness; cheating by servants; death of friend (as it is the eighth from the eleventh); many friends among the working class of people. If well aspected, good and faithful servants. If the *ruler* of the *sixth* is in the eighth and afflicted, a death in the family shortly. No luck with animals. *Saturn* in the sixth, trouble with animals and cattle. *Mars* here, danger of fevers, which may cause surgery; dangerous sickness; death of pets, small animals or servants.

Jupiter here, gain and honor through service, employment or practice of healing; may study hygiene, medicine, healing, etc. The querent may possess healing abilities or probably will gain through law (as the sixth is the tenth from the ninth). *Venus*, profit in animals and cattle; sickness through over-indulgence if Venus is afflicted by Uranus, Saturn or Mars. Fondness for pets and small animals. Venus here afflicted, the person usually marries below his station mentally or socially, or will have a sickly partner. The *Sun* here, mental uneasiness; proud, wasteful servants; and long sickness, unless the *Sun* is in good aspect to Jupiter or Venus.

The *Part of Fortune* or *Dragon's Head*, good servants and gain through service. *Mercury* here afflicted, trouble through blood relatives; probably some severe illness. *Many planets* in this house, much sickness; many private enemies, especially if the ruler of the twelfth is in the sixth house.

Seventh House Questions

Answers questions concerning marriage; lawsuits; whether property loss will be recovered; the lover; description of the person the querent will marry; theft and description of the thief; fugitives or runaways; offenders, escaped from justice; grandfathers, being the fourth from the fourth; whether it is best to move; contracts; whether contracts are favorable; speculation in funds, shares, etc.; whether to buy or sell at certain times; partnership in trade and business; fines; in battle, who is victorious; war questions; children of the brother or sister, being the fifth from the third; the physician; defendants in law suits; third brother or sister; the second child; all people with whom we have common dealings. It signifies the astrologer.

Planets in the Seventh House

Neptune in the seventh usually does not give desire for the usual domestic marriage, but in trine or sextile of the Sun, Moon or Venus, would bring a union more of the soul; or one might marry a genius. The square or opposition indicates jealousy and scandal, and often perverted attachments; trouble through deceit and treachery; also through lawsuits, sickness; and trouble through women. Neptune here well aspected gives popularity; love for science, especially occult science; interest in magic.

Uranus here, afflicting the Moon or ruler of the seventh, disappointment in courtship; unhappy marriage; either the wife or husband will be difficult to please.

Saturn, marriage is delayed; probably disagreement between the parties; many enemies. Saturn here afflicted or peregrine, a poor husband or wife. Saturn close to the cusp of the seventh in opposition or square to the Sun shows falls, bruises and much sickness. Saturn exalted or well aspected, gain through all seventh house affairs; honorable marriage.

Jupiter here, a good husband or wife; agreeable courtship; marriage to a stranger with education, but trouble with relatives, especially if Mercury afflicts Jupiter.

Mars here, many quarrels; lawsuits; public enemies; a bad husband or wife; disappointment in courtship; a lover given to change. If Mars afflicts the Sun or Uranus, the lover will prove unfaithful. Mars here, square or opposition to the Moon, danger by fire, or by violence or suicide; fondness for the opposite sex; martial unhappiness.

Sun here, honorable marriage; public recognition; the square or opposition of Mars, Saturn or Uranus brings trouble and attacks from powerful people; these aspects bring great anxiety, enmity, and discord.

Venus here, a moderate wife; square the Moon or Neptune, careless; but this is a fortunate place for Venus as she is in her own house. A planet in its own house or exaltation is as one in his own home. Few public enemies.

Mercury here denotes many moves and changes; a good but fussy wife; attraction to younger people; probable marriage as a result of a journey, or to one of kin. If Mercury is afflicted by Mars, difficulty with disreputable women, and sickness.

Moon here, many changes of residence; trine to Jupiter or Venus, happy marriage. Moon here badly aspected, death of the marriage partner.

Dragon's Head, fortunate; *Dragon's Tail*, the reverse, and many enemies. *Part of Fortune*, the husband or wife will be wealthy; gain through all seventh house affairs.

Many planets in the seventh house, anxiety about husband, lover or wife; unhappy if married. If the ruler of the first is stronger or less afflicted than the ruler of the seventh, the querent overcomes his enemies; but if the ruler of the seventh is stronger, they will overcome him. Good aspect or mutual reception between the rulers of the first and seventh shows a desire for marriage; and also shows harmony between man and wife.

Eighth House Questions

Answers questions concerning deaths; legacies; wills; escrows; retirement money premiums; old age pensions; money of the partner, wife, husband or public enemy, being the second from the seventh labor; sorrow; relatives of servants, being the third from the sixth; sickness of brothers or sisters, being the sixth from the third; also the substance of a third brother or sister, as the seventh represents the third brother or sister.

Planets in the Eighth House

Neptune in the eighth, wills and money of the marriage partner bring worry and anxiety. When badly aspected, trance conditions; many misfortunes; trouble through deceased persons.

The *ruler* of the eighth afflicted or retrograde in the eighth, the querent has loaned money that he will never recover. If the cusp of the eighth house is Aries, Scorpio or Capricorn, danger of a violent death.

Uranus here afflicted by the rulers of the first and sixth gives strange diseases in whatever part of the body is signified by the signs these planets are in.

Saturn here, doubtful legacies; if in bad aspect to the Sun and Moon, will bring delay and worry over wills and legacies; probably a long, lingering death. Saturn here well aspected, gain and honor in handling the estate and money of others' inheritance and insurance. Probably work of governmental nature.

Jupiter gives hopes of a legacy and gain by marriage; a peaceful death. Gain through seventh house affairs. Afflicted, death of the partner's kindred; persecution regarding religion; trouble through publications. The *North Node* or *Part of Fortune*, the same as Jupiter.

Mars here shows violent death; loss of substance; want of money; trouble with lovers or partners over money matters.

Venus here, a natural death; gain by marriage. Venus or Jupiter here afflicted, bank failures; also the querent will suffer by reputedly honest persons.

Moon here, many changes in residence; square or opposition of the Sun, Mars, Saturn or Uranus, danger of surgical operations or serious accidents.

Every care should be taken when Mars transits these planets or this house or the sign Scorpio.

Ninth House Questions

Answers questions concerning the safety, profit and success of voyages and long distance travel; the clergy; preferment in the church; success of books; insurance; science and learning; insurance indemnities; blood relations of the wife or husband, being the third from the seventh; health of the father or mother, being the sixth from the fourth; grand-children, being the fifth from the fifth; the third child; the fourth brother or sister.

Planets in the Ninth House

Neptune in the ninth, the mind is visionary and psychic; difficulty with relatives; the square or opposition of the Sun or Venus takes the loved one to some far-off country; also fraud by trustees or lawyers. In bad aspect to the Moon and Mercury, Neptune in this house gives evil imagination.

Uranus here, publishing; teaching; fond of science; loves to travel. Square or opposition of the Sun or Mercury, long journeys and much traveling by sea; a romantic mind. Many friends through travel and learning.

Saturn here, rather bad for journeys; honorable friends; just mind. The sextile or trine of the Sun or Moon to Saturn brings responsible position in far-off countries.

Jupiter here unafflicted, good disposition; happiness and success through ninth house affairs. Many fine qualities. If afflicted, difficulties with relatives, science and religious matters.

Mars here, a religious bigot; losses at sea; quarrels with the partner's relatives.

Venus in the ninth afflicted, very immodest, inquisitive. If well aspected, music and fine arts attract the mind; gentle, cultured intellect. Conjunction the Moon in cardinal or mutable signs, long voyages, with love of the sea. The weather always favors those who have Venus well placed in the ninth house.

Mercury here, science; invention; fond of travel; in cardinal or common signs in aspect to Mars, Moon or Uranus, will bring many journeys and interest in travel; in good aspect to Jupiter, love of knowledge, science and religion; to Saturn or Neptune, mysticism. Mercury conjunction the Sun is weak here; mind rather contracted and superficial.

The *Moon* here, especially in movable signs, much journeying to far-off countries; trine or sextile of Sun, Saturn or Jupiter, great success in a foreign country; trine, sextile or conjunct Venus, money from relatives by marriage; in aspect to Neptune, the mind is visionary; many strange dreams.

The *ruler* of the *ninth* just falling from the cusp, the querent is on a journey, probably one of pleasure of visiting. The ruler of the fourth in the ninth afflicted, a parent, probably the father, is afflicted, and if it is Uranus that afflicts, the parent has impaired memory, and his nervous system is weakened. The rulers of the first and ninth in good aspect, the person will do well as a merchant, scholar or traveler.

Tenth House Questions

Answers questions concerning kings, presidents or masters; honor; gaining of office appointment or employment; business situations; the mother-in-law or father-in-law, being the fourth from the seventh; the business for which a person is best suited; substance taken away by thieves, being the fourth from the seventh; children of servants or tenants, being the fifth from the sixth; private enemies of friends, being the twelfth of the eleventh; counting the eleventh as the first, sickness of the children, being the sixth from the fifth; what we are able to gain through science, publishing, voyages, arts; also denotes the father or mother of the querent.

Planets in the Tenth House

Study well the planets in this house, as it predicts most important matters.

Neptune in the tenth, not a good position for worldly success or power unless it is well placed by sign and well aspected. A good aspect to the Sun or Moon would bring a career under strange circumstances with an element of danger to the name and reputation. An opposition from the fourth house would bring either trouble or sadness from the parents, or sudden loss by death of one of them. Many worries in the home life. In good aspect to the Sun, Moon and Venus gives gain and success by some curious means. It strongly attracts to mysticism.

Uranus here shows a person has more than one business, or changes from one to another, with danger of sudden loss unless Uranus is well aspected. Trine or sextile of the Sun and Moon, comes through all difficulties with honor; in good aspect to Mercury, gives talent as a writer of romantic fiction; with Venus, clever actor or artist; gain and honor through those of high standing.

Saturn here, if in evil aspect, dishonor, danger of imprisonment; with Mercury square or opposition, especially if either planet is retrograde, the honor is attacked; if the Sun is also in bad aspect, loss of one's reputation. Saturn here in air signs, danger from heights that cause death; afflicted, all affairs go wrong.

Jupiter here, success, prosperous trade, wealth and honor; conjunct Sun, lasting honor. In good aspect to the Sun, Moon, Venus or Mercury, gives much wisdom allied with common sense, and makes a splendid judge of character. Jupiter here well aspected helps one out of all difficulties.

Mars here, fond of warlike proceedings, and may be given to violence; but well aspected, brings much success. In Scorpio, makes clever sailors, doctors, surgeons; in Leo or Aries, famous soldiers; in Sagittarius, engineers, teachers, travelers; in air signs in good aspect to the Sun, Venus or Mercury, artists, musicians, novelists. Mars in the tenth house gives constructive skill and manual dexterity, especially in earth signs; afflicted here it gives conceit, push, boldness, bad temper; conjunct the Moon, scandal.

Sun here, honor and assistance from respectable people; a rising fortune. Honorable children; luck in speculation or enterprise.

Venus here, much success to any venture; very fortunate unless in bad aspect to Saturn, then the querent will be mean in conduct. If well aspected, gain through the opposite sex. Conjunct Mercury or conjunct, trine or sextile Moon, a successful artistic career. In cardinal signs, eminence and fame. Venus here well aspected the person will be much loved during the whole course of life. Venus here and afflicting Uranus, very shallow abilities; also public disgrace and scandal if in bad aspect to Mars.

Mercury in the tenth in an airy sign or common sign (Virgo), well aspected by parallel, conjunction, trine or sextile of the Moon would make a great scholar and will possess much eloquence; in good aspect to Mars, penetration, a quick mind; to Jupiter, good judgment. Mercury here with these aspects to Uranus gives fortune and success in literature or a professional career. Mercury conjunction the Sun, business would interest most, especially if there is at the same time a good aspect to Saturn. But Mercury here without aspect or afflicted gives a restless spirit with great changeability. The name and honor are severely criticized.

Moon here, gain in possessions by trade, profession, public or government work. This is a critical position for the Moon if afflicted by a square or opposition of Mars, it brings scandal; by Uranus, accidents and great losses; by Saturn, would impede the career in every way, bringing loss of credit and reputation; by Neptune, no continuity, but changes and misfortunes.

The ruler of the tenth and first in good aspect, success in all tenth house affairs.

Eleventh House Questions

Answers questions concerning friends, hopes and wishes; trusts; flatterers; what we may expect and what we desire; whether friends are true or false; advisers; aviation; group circumstances; it is the substance of whatever the tenth house promises, being the second from the tenth; sickness of servants, tenants, aunts or uncles, being the sixth from the sixth; death of the father or mother, being the eighth from the fourth; our fifth brother or sister; the fourth child.

Planets in the Eleventh House

Neptune in the eleventh conjunct the Sun, Moon or Venus, care should be taken how one trusts the opinion of friends; Neptune here afflicted is a warning of treachery and evil motives, bringing strange friends not of one's own class. Badly aspected, deceitful friends.

Uranus here trine or sextile Mercury, Moon, Venus or Sun brings many friends that are helpful, sincere, clever and original. Badly aspected, impulsive and unreliable friends.

Saturn here, false friends; death of children; disappointment of hopes and wishes. In good aspect to the Sun or Moon, powerful friends; in good aspect with Mercury or Venus, loving and intellectual friends.

Jupiter here, true friends; riches; happiness; association with those in higher positions; many hopes and wishes fulfilled.

Mars, false friends; wicked children.

Sun here, happiness and good friends; Saturn older, Mercury younger, Venus women, Mars men; cardinal signs, well known or famous people; fixed signs, unchanging friendship; common signs, ability to get on well with most people, and to find friendly influence in all classes.

Venus here, honorable and faithful friends, especially women. Good aspect to Moon or Jupiter, fondness for social life; popular.

Mercury here, deceitful friends unless well aspected; also friendship or association with literary people; friends through journeys; much correspondence with friends.

Moon in the eleventh, friendship of women. Afflicted, trouble and unhappiness through friendships, and children.

If the *ruler* of the eleventh is in the eleventh unafflicted, good and sincere friends; if in good aspect to the ruler of the first, friends will be permanent and advantageous.

Twelfth House Questions

Answers questions concerning large cattle; suicide; assassinations; disappointments; sorrow; affliction; imprisonment; persecution; malice; secret enemies; enforced labor; hospitals; asylums; blood relatives on the mother's side, being the third from the tenth; banished persons. The substance of friends, being the second from the eleventh; sickness of wives or husbands, being the sixth from the seventh; death of children, being the eighth from the fifth; our brother's or sister's trade and honor, being the tenth from the third when we count the third as the first house of the brother or sister; enemies of servants or tenants, being the seventh from the sixth—also where the tenant will go if he moves; the mother's first brother or sister, being the third from the tenth; also short journeys of the mother, master or mistress.

Planets in the Twelfth House

Neptune in the twelfth, very mediumistic; many anxieties; powerless enemies; secret investigation; limitations; afflictions and sorrows prove a blessing in disguise by developing inner growth and understanding. The Moon conjunction Neptune, a religious nature.

Uranus here or near the cusp, clever in his business; enemies of a public character; unexpected jealousies; sorrowful friends; good friendship among occult people.

Saturn here, trouble; persecution by false friends; business associates become secret enemies; professional secrets; all limitations relieved by study of the occult or new thought.

Jupiter, few enemies and victory over them; secret investigation. Limitations prove a blessing by developing understanding.

Mars here, bold and daring enemies; danger of imprisonment, especially if in bad aspect to the Sun, Moon or Saturn; also liable to accidents to the feet. *Sun* here afflicted, many enemies; children cause secret sorrow.

Venus here, fond of animals; enemies unable to do him harm. If afflicted, unhappy marriage; secret sorrow and jealousy.

Mercury gives mischief and scandalous reports if in bad aspect to Saturn and Mars. Well aspected to the Moon and Uranus, gain through occultism and psyches.

Moon in the twelfth, the person's health is affected by the parents taking journeys; also suffers sorrow through one or both of them. Probably hindered in early education due to sickness.

Sun here afflicted brings sorrow, self-undoing, especially if the same sign of the zodiac occupies the first and twelfth houses. Children cause secret sorrow; ruin through speculations. *Sun* here square Saturn, and Saturn in the tenth house, danger of imprisonment.

But the Moon in good aspect to the Sun or the Sun parallel, conjunction, sextile or trine to Jupiter, would bring success and steady improvement as life advances; also gain through investigation of the occult.

The *ruler* of the twelfth in the first, or the ruler of the first in the twelfth, much sorrow and anxiety of mind. If the ruler of the first is in good aspect to the ruler of the twelfth from the fourth, sixth, eighth or twelfth there will be enemies in the guise of friends.

Whether the Question is Radical or Fit to be Judged

The astrologer should always be sure that the chart is radical. It is not considered radical when the degree on the eastern horizon, or first house, is less than a three-degree orb unless this degree and sign should be the same as in the natal chart of the person who asked the question.

If more than twenty-seven degrees of a sign rises, it is not considered safe to judge the chart unless this degree and sign also ties up with the person's natal chart. These rules will not have to be considered in an event happening or in any election charts.

Be very careful in your judgment when the cusp of the sixth house is afflicted, or the ruler of the seventh cusp is retrograde. It is an argument that the judgment of the astrologer will not give satisfaction and may not be correct. Retrograde planets never give all that is expected.

When the testimonies of good and bad are equal, use the Table of the Dignities and Debilities of Planets and judge accordingly. But only do so if the Moon makes one or more aspects before it leaves the sign it is in when the question is asked.

Horary Questions by House

First House Questions

What Part of Life Is Likely to Be Fortunate?

Life begins with the hour of birth. The younger days are judged from the Ascendant to the tenth house cusp, the period from one to twenty-one years of age; from the tenth house to the eighth, from twenty-one to thirty-five years; from the seventh to the fifth, thirty-five to fifty years; from the fourth to the first, from fifty years to the end of life.

Wherever Jupiter and Venus are posited usually denotes the most prosperous years, and if these planets are on the angles, there is promise of preferment and great honor that makes the life interesting and successful.

Ptolemy says, "If the ruler of the ascendant or a planet in the first is a benefic, and the Sun and Moon are conjunct, or in good aspect to good planets, and if these luminaries are in opposition from the first to the seventh house, the person will be highly prosperous in all things, health included; but the contrary effect will be produced should a malefic be on the ascendant."

Duration of Physical Life

The duration of the physical life is dependent on the Sun, Moon and Ascendant. If the degree rising and the Sun and Moon are free from the parallel, conjunction, square or opposition to the ruler of the fourth, sixth, eighth or twelfth houses—this denotes a long life.

If the querent's significators are in their dignities, in good houses, and increasing in light and motion and well aspected, long life is indicated. If the ruler or co-ruler of the Ascendant is in the first or the benefic planets are in any good aspect to the degree rising, long life is shown. In judging the aspect between the Sun and Moon to Saturn, Mars, Uranus and Neptune, it is important to notice which are in elevation, especially those in square, parallel or opposition.

If Saturn is in the eighth house in opposition to the Moon in the second house, then Saturn is elevated above the Moon. This aspect with the malefic elevated would not give much hope in the case of severe illness.

This rule also applies to the Sun and the malefics. If Uranus is in a cardinal sign in the twelfth house in square aspect to the Sun in the fourth, Uranus being elevated, it would bring unexpected, sudden disaster to the fourth house and all it stands for.

Neptune elevated in Aries in the tenth house in opposition to Venus in the fourth would bring despair and deepest sorrow in love matters and other things denoted by Venus, which would end unhappily in some strange and mysterious manner and usually beyond our power to control.

But should the Sun or Moon be in the eighth and Saturn in the second in opposition, there would be every chance of recovery in illness. This would be true in a like manner of the other malefics.

Fixed stars of the nature of Mars, Saturn or Uranus in the first or any planet peregrine or in the Via combust degree and retrograde in the first endangers the life.

In all questions pertaining to how long a person is likely to live, the natal chart of the person asking the question or of the person enquired about should be consulted.

Death is always due to a train of evil aspects, directions and transits to the hyleg and other vital points. If the hyleg is not afflicted we have reason to believe the person will enjoy long life.

The Ascendant or its ruler, Jupiter, Venus or Mercury well aspected in the eighth or to the ruler of the cusp of the eighth, the person usually dies a natural death.

The Nature of Death

The nature of death should be judged chiefly by the secondary directions operating at the time.

The first house signifies life, the sixth house sickness, the eighth house death, the twelfth house self-undoing, etc.

If these rulers are malefics or malefics are in these houses and afflicted, the person will probably not live long.

The nature of any event taking place or likely to occur can be ascertained by observing the aspects which the Moon last formed and from what the ruler of the Ascendant has last separated, considering both the planets and the aspect; this will show what has taken place according to the houses in which they formed the aspects and of which they are the rulers.

Their next application will show what to expect; if these aspects are evil, judge evil; if they are good, then it will be fortunate.

Good and evil attending life should always be judged from the chart in general. The student may obtain more definite information by studying the chapter on the planets in the houses.

Where Shall He Go to Better Himself

If a person is dissatisfied or unfortunate where he is and wishes to make a change and asks which way he should go to better himself, find out if there is any particular purpose or object in mind for the change because he should follow the significator of such purpose.

If health should be the object, follow the ruler of the first and the Moon, provided this first is not a malefic and afflicted; if money matters, the ruler of the second and the Part of Fortune should be followed; if honor, business promotion, etc. consider the tenth house and the Sun and follow those that are the strongest and best dignified.

If none are strong or fortunate, either by house, sign or aspect, then he should remain where he is and try to do something constructive about it.

Suppose when the question was asked about a change, the ruler of the first was in the ninth house in the sign of Aries and fortunately aspected. The querent should be advised to go south-east; Aries is an eastern sign and the ninth house is south-west. Combining the house and sign gives us south-east. Follow these rules for questions of this nature.

Questions Concerning an Absent Person

The person who asks the question will be represented by the rising sign and its ruler. The person inquired about is generally a blood relation or friend and should be read accordingly.

But if there is no relationship, etc., then take the seventh house to denote the absent person's first house; the eighth, his second or money; the ninth, his third or brethren and travel; the tenth, his fourth or the home, father or mother; the eleventh, his fifth or children and love affairs; the twelfth, his sixth or sickness, work, and servants; the first, his seventh or the wife or husband or sweetheart; the second, his eighth or death and other people's money; the third, his ninth or journeys and travel; the fourth, his tenth or honor, mother or father, and trade; the fifth, his eleventh or hopes, wishes and friends; the sixth, his twelfth or confinement (hospital or prison) and private enemies.

If the ruler of the seventh is applying to a conjunction or bad aspect of the ruler of the eighth, he is probably near death, and, if the aspect is separating and there is no help from a benefic, he has probably ceased to exist for as many days, weeks or months as there are degrees between these rulers.

If the ruler of the seventh is in the fourth and the Moon is in square aspect, there is danger of death. The Moon in Aries or the ruler of the first parallel or conjunction the ruler of the eighth or fourth, he is dead; or in the sixth, he may die. The ruler of the seventh or the Moon in the eighth or fourth, Via Combust, the person is dead.

If the ruler of the seventh or the Moon separates from the ruler of the sixth or eighth and makes no benefic aspect to a benefic planet, then he is in great danger and will probably remain so.

But if the ruler of the seventh separates from the ruler of the sixth or eighth and applies to any of the benefics by parallel or any good aspect, say he will soon recover.

If the ruler of the seventh separates from a bad aspect to the ruler of the twelfth or its cusp, he has been confined or in jail or in serious trouble.

Ship at Sea and Its Voyage

The various parts of a ship are ruled much the same as the parts or members of a man's body:

Aries—the breast or prow of a ship

Taurus—under the breast, toward the water

Gemini—the rudder or stern-post

Cancer—the bottom or floor of the ship

Leo—the top of the ship above the water

Virgo—the belly of the ship

Libra—that part above the breast in the water

Scorpio—where the sailors live

Sagittarius—the sailors

Capricorn—the end or stern of the ship

Aquarius—the Captain or Master

Pisces—all the parts that make the ship navigate: oars or wheels, engines, diesel motors, etc.

The Ascendant and the Moon signify the vessel and cargo. The ruler of the Ascendant denotes those who sail in her.

When all these are fortunate, they signify that the ship is safe; on the contrary, if they are afflicted, the vessel and all in her are in real danger, if not lost.

A malefic planet located in the first; the ruler of the Ascendant in the eighth in bad aspect with either the ruler of the fourth, sixth, twelfth or eighth; or the Moon combust, under the earth; all these are indications of loss to the ship.

If the Ascendant and the Moon are unfortunate and the ruler of the first is fortunate, the ship is lost but the men are saved.

When the Moon is fortunate, and the ruler of the first is unfortunate, then the vessel will do well or is safe, but her crew are in danger of death by the ship fever or some epidemic disease.

These rules apply when she is on her voyage and the querent is anxiously serious to know how the ship is or has fared. But to know the result of a voyage, we must investigate the figure as follows:

Will the Voyage Prove Prosperous?

If the fortunate planets and the Moon are in the ninth, tenth, first, fourth or seventh, or the ruler of the first is well located, or the rulers of the first and ninth are well situated, then the voyage will be prosperous.

But if Uranus, Saturn, Mars, Neptune or the South Node is in the above places or in succedent houses, the ship will meet with some misfortune in that part of the ship, or to those persons signified by the sign where the malefic is located.

Saturn afflicting the first and the Moon denotes sickness, shipwreck, enemies; Mars shows fire, fever and capture, if no good aspects of the benefics intervene; the South Node much the same as Mars.

If the ruler of the first in this case is free from affliction and strong, the crew will escape; if the rulers of the angles are free from affliction, and the ruler of the first also, most of the cargo and crew will be saved.

If the tenth house is afflicted by Mars, and near violent fixed stars, Mars being at the same time in Gemini, Virgo or Aquarius, the ship will be in danger of being burned by the enemy. But if Mars is in the tenth and not in the above human signs, then the ship will be in danger of fire by lightening, accident or explosion.

Again, if a square or opposition exists between the ruler of the first and the disposer of the Moon, there will then arise discord and contention among the seamen, or there will be so much dispute between the captain and his crew as often to cause open mutiny.

In this case, the strongest significator will overcome; that is, if the ruler of the first is better dignified than the disposer of the Moon, the men will overcome; but if the disposer of the Moon is stronger than the ruler of the first, then the captain will prevail, and the crew will be satisfied.

Will the Voyage Be Long or Short?

The ruler of the ninth oriental or a planet in the ninth, swift or in a movable sign, denotes the voyage to be short and quick; but if occidental, long and tedious; if in common signs, a reasonable time, and the ship may land at a different port from the one originally intended.

The ruler of the ninth and the Moon and the ruler of the first in fixed signs denotes a long voyage; Taurus, Virgo or Capricorn on the Ascendant shows the voyage will be rather dull.

If the ruler of the first is retrograde or either it or the Moon applies to a retrograde planet, it signifies the person that goes on the voyage will return in a short time, or perhaps before he reaches the place intended. Jupiter or Venus in the tenth denotes mirth, pleasure; in the ninth, health and fair weather.

Of Bills and Promissory Notes

The first and the Moon signify the querent; the second, the Part of Fortune and the ruler of the second, the bill. The seventh and its ruler denote the quesited; the eighth, his money.

If the ruler of the seventh or eighth afflicts the Part of Fortune or the ruler of the second, there is reason to fear the bill will not be paid.

The presence of Uranus, Saturn, Mars, Mercury or the South Node in the second, unless the planets so located are well aspected by the ruler of the seventh or eighth, or by the Part of Fortune, Venus or the Moon, from the seventh, tenth or eleventh, the bill will be dishonored.

If the Part of Fortune receives any evil aspect of the ruler of the first, it will not be paid. If the Part of Fortune receives a good aspect from the ruler of the first, seventh or eighth, it will be paid.

Note: At the time of signing a bill, etc. be sure that the Part of Fortune, Mercury, Uranus or Neptune are not afflicted in the second, seventh, or eighth, for this indicates fraud. The Part of Fortune always denotes gain if unafflicted.

Your principle significators are the rulers of the first, second, seventh, eighth and fourth and the Part of Fortune. Then look to the planet that may afflict or assist your significators. Unless the affliction comes from the seventh, eighth, or eleventh house, it need not be feared.

The South Node in the fourth denotes evil to the firm in question. Uranus, Saturn or Mars afflicted near the cusp of the fourth shows the firm to be unfortunate, especially if the ruler of the fourth is affected. A benefic planet in the fourth, well aspected by the Sun, Moon or ruler of the seventh or eighth, the firm will prosper.

In order to judge the condition of the parties with whom you do business, look well to the planets aspecting the rulers of the seventh and fourth.

If there are many planets well aspected, the firm is doing well and will be able to meet all demands. If malefic planets make bad aspects to the rulers of the fourth, seventh and eighth, judge the firm will suffer loss through the parties described by the planet afflicting.

But if the rulers of the fourth, seventh and eighth are in their dignities, it will not go to ruin but will compromise. The evil aspects of Neptune, Uranus and Mercury to the significators are indicative of forgery or fraud.

Second House Questions

Whether the Querent Will Gain All He Expects

The first house, its ruler and the Moon denote the querent.

The second house, its ruler or planet in the second denotes the substance or money of the querent.

The seventh house and its ruler represent the debtor or person with whom you wish to do business.

The eighth house and its ruler show his means of paying.

The questions can be regarding money loaned, such as debts, the opening of bank accounts, lending of money to another person, money received from goods delivered, etc.

It will be obtained if the ruler of the first or the Moon is in good aspect or parallel to the ruler of the eighth and this ruler unafflicted by the malefics; or if the ruler of the first or the Moon is parallel or conjunct Venus or Jupiter and if either of these planets is in an angle unafflicted or in the eighth house; if the querent's ruler is parallel or conjunct Venus or Jupiter and these planets dignified; if the ruler of the eighth is well aspected to Venus or Jupiter in the first or second, in mutual reception or applying to each other in any good aspect; or if the Moon translates the light from the ruler of the seventh to the ruler of the first or applies to any good aspect.

Expect disappointment if the ruler of the first is Via combust or retrograde or if it makes no good aspect to the ruler of the seventh or eighth, even if the ruler of the seventh and eighth is Venus or Jupiter.

The querent will be disappointed in gaining what he asks if the Moon is in bad aspect to Mercury or if the ruler of the first should be Mercury retrograde.

The South Node, Uranus, Saturn or Mars in the eighth or the ruler of the eighth in the first or seventh in their detriment, fall, peregrine, retrograde or opposition with the ruler of the seventh shows disappointment.

The ruler of the seventh or eighth in the first or second, not in mutual reception to the ruler of the first or second or the Moon, or square to each other; the ruler of the eighth or seventh applying to a bad aspect of the ruler of the first or second, Moon or the Part of Fortune, the quesited is a cheat and has no good intention toward the querent.

It is said that a malefic planet interposing, or an evil aspect, shows the cause or person from whom the trouble arises, by the house such planet rules, at the time of the question.

Instructions

Instead of taking the ruler of the seventh and eighth: For the recovery of wages, take the rulers of the tenth and eleventh; for asking of the father, take the rulers of the fourth and fifth; for asking of a brother, sister or neighbor, take rulers of the third and fourth; for asking of a friend, take the rulers of the eleventh and twelfth.

By this means you may go around the chart, only remember that the succeeding house signifies his substance to that which is his Ascendant.

Of Riches or Gain

The significators of riches are the second, its ruler, the planets therein, the Part of Fortune, and its dispositor.

The querent will be rich if these are strongly dignified, free from affliction, well aspected by the benefics, or in reception with them. Pay close attention to the dispositor of the Part of Fortune and the first application it receives or makes.

If the rulers of the first and second are in mutual reception, or in good aspect with each other, or the ruler of the first is in the second, or the ruler of the second is in the first—this is a strong testimony of gain.

If the Moon applies to the ruler of the second, either by conjunction or good aspect from good houses in the figure; if the Moon is in her dignities in the second, in conjunction, sextile or trine Jupiter or Venus or the Part of Fortune; if the Moon or any other planet translates the light of the ruler of the second to the ruler of the first, then he will gain wealth.

The Part of Fortune in the first shows gain by his own industry. The disposer of the Part of Fortune well aspected, free from affliction, is a sign of riches, especially in the first or tenth.

The best sign of riches is the rulers of the first and second and Jupiter joined together in the second, tenth, seventh, fourth or eleventh. The next best testimony is their application to a sextile or trine, with reception.

Many planets angular, swift in motion, is good. The majority of planets direct in good houses and each having some accidental dignity is also good.

Jupiter, who naturally signifies riches, or Venus, or the North Node, free from bad aspects, denotes rich and if this happens in fixed signs, so much the better.

The Sun and Moon in sextile or trine from good houses is a symbol of riches and honor, especially if they are essentially dignified.

Testimonies of Poverty

Uranus, Saturn, Mars or the South Node in the second, peregrine, retrograde or afflicting the ruler of the second, Jupiter, Venus or the Part of Fortune, either by body or aspect, is a sign of poverty.

Many planets badly aspected in the second is a sign of poverty. The Sun, Mars or the South Node in the second shows waste of the estate already possessed. The Sun in bad aspect to Jupiter denotes extravagance.

When the significators of substance apply to each other by square or opposition, if they are in mutual reception, may show the acquiring of riches, but it will be with great difficulty; neither will he take good care of the substances he may then possess.

By What Means Will the Querent Obtain Riches?

If you have found that the querent will obtain wealth you may know how and by what means, by using the following rules:

The ruler of the second in the first, especially if well aspected by Uranus, shows gain without much labor.

If the ruler of the second or the Moon promise substance by mutual aspect, observe from what house the aspect is, or what house the Moon rules; if neither of these is the promiser of substance, see in what house the Part of Fortune and its dispositor are placed.

If the planet assisting is in the first, the querent will gain by his own effort; or if poor, he will gain by labor or by care or invention.

But if the assisting planet is not ruler of the second, he will gain by managing his own affairs, etc. or by such things as are of the nature of that planet, the sign he is in being also considered.

The ruler of the second in the third, or the rulers of these houses in good aspect with each other, shows that his wealth will be derived from his neighbor or kindred or by inland journeys.

The ruler of the second in the fourth, fortunately placed in good aspect of the ruler of the fourth, and not afflicted as before mentioned, the querent will obtain riches by his father, or by lands or houses purchased, or by money loaned by his relatives.

The ruler of the second in the fifth, and in good aspect of the ruler of the fifth, shows gain by cards, racing, gaming or other amusements, cafes, places of recreation, all things connected with theaters, and such things as the fifth house denotes.

The ruler of the second in the sixth shows gain by workmen, servants, dealing in small cattle, physic affairs, stewardships, and things denoted by the sixth house.

The ruler of the second in the seventh denotes gain by women, wives, bargains, lawsuits, war or commerce.

The ruler of the eighth making the aspect denotes legacies, or a wife's portion, or gain by traveling to some country where he will settle and become rich unexpectedly, especially if the planet should be Uranus.

The ruler of the ninth indicates riches by voyages, the wife's relations, or by some lawyer or clergyman, or by religious professions or learning.

If Cancer or Pisces is on the ninth, he may gain by a voyage; but if Taurus, Virgo or Capricorn is on the ninth, he should remove to those places denoted by those signs and by dealing in such commodities as that country produces.

The ruler of the tenth promises gain by holding office under the government, or by any mechanical profession.

If the querent is young, he should learn those businesses that may be shown by the sign and planet in the tenth or its rulers.

The eleventh and its ruler give unexpected benefits by recommendation of friends, men in power and unexpected good fortune.

The fortunate aspect cast from the twelfth increases the querent's substance by horses or great cattle; or if the sign is Gemini or Aquarius, by means of prisons, as a jailor or sheriff's officer or detective; if the sign is Aries, Taurus or Capricorn, by cattle, horse racing; if Virgo, by produce.

Note: The student must be careful in observing to answer these questions by the same rules with which he answered the first question—that is, whether the querent would be rich or poor.

Also be careful to keep in mind the rules at the head of these inquiries, namely the rulers of these houses or planets therein casting a good aspect to the rulers of the first or second, or the Part of Fortune or the Moon, or the dispositor of the Part of Fortune.

Cause of Poverty or Hindrance of Gain

If the figure denies riches, see if the evil arises from the planet or planets afflicting the ruler of the first, second, the Moon or the Part of Fortune or its dispositor.

If the ruler of the first afflicts, the querent is his own ruin; if the ruler of the second, he is poor and cannot help it; if the ruler of the third, he will be kept poor by frequent removals, poor relations, or by some neighbor underselling him.

Wherever the South Node is will always show the cause of loss or poverty, according to the house it occupies. Also, Jupiter or Venus may be hindered by being afflicted, for every planet must denote the work for which he is by nature best fitted.

The South Node in the ninth house gives less trouble, as the person is helped through the higher mind or religion.

The Time When the Querent May Attain Riches

Note the application of the Moon, or the ruler of the first, has to the planets signifying the substance of the querent. See how many degrees they are distant from each other, and so judge of weeks, months, or years, as they are angular, etc.; fixed, etc.

Will the Querent Receive His Wages or Salary?

The ruler of the first and the Moon signify the querent; the tenth signifies the person who pays the salary; the eleventh signifies the salary paid.

The foregoing rules will answer this; remember that instead of taking the ruler of the seventh and eighth, you take the rulers of the tenth and eleventh for the quesited.

The rulers of the first, tenth, eleventh and second in good aspect with each other, the salary will be paid.

The ruler of the first or the Moon conjunction the ruler of the eleventh in the eleventh; the ruler of the first in good aspect with the ruler of the eleventh; the Moon in good aspect with either the ruler of the tenth or eleventh; all these show it will be paid.

The time of receiving is indicated by the number of degrees between the ruler of the first and the Moon and the ruler of the eleventh.

Third House Questions

Of Absent Brothers, Sisters, Cousins, Neighbors, Children of Friends, etc.

The first, its ruler and the Moon are taken for the querent.

The third and its ruler are taken to signify the absent one. Consider well the third and the condition of the ruler of the third as well as the Moon.

The third house becomes the first of the question.

The ruler of the third in conjunction or bad aspect with Uranus, Saturn, Mars or the South Node shows that the condition of the brother is sorrowful; if it is in the third unafflicted, then he is well, but if the ruler of the third is in the third afflicted, he may be in health, but is perplexed and much worried.

The brother is sick or dead if the Moon and ruler of the third are in opposition to the ruler of the eighth from the second and eighth, or from the sixth and twelfth houses. Also, if the ruler of the third is afflicted in the twelfth by the ruler of the eighth and tenth and if the Moon is ruler in this case and afflicted by Uranus, then say the brother is drowned.

Great danger of death if the ruler of the third is in the fourth square the Moon in the seventh. If you find the ruler of the third and the Moon combust in the natural fourth or eighth or joined with the ruler of the eighth, then the quesited is dead.

The ruler of the third in the first house, unafflicted, shows he is among friends, but there in conjunction of Uranus, Neptune, Saturn, Mars or the South Node, then his friends are deceivers, and he has no hope of success.

The first is the eleventh from the third; therefore, the friends of the brother.

The ruler of the third in the second, especially if retrograde or in its fall or detriment, he is in great sorrow of mind and will move from his present place as soon as possible; but if his ruler is much afflicted, he is then confined in prison or hospital. The second is the twelfth from the third; therefore, it is the house of sorrow.

If the ruler of the third is in the third house, free from affliction, then say he is in health; but afflicted without mutual reception, he is dissatisfied and wishes to move from his present place.

The ruler of the third in the fourth, without bad aspects to the malefics, the quesited intends getting rich where he is; but if afflicted, he will never gain much property. In the fifth, in conjunction with the ruler of the fifth, it shows the absent brother to be in health and happily situated; but if the ruler of the third is void of course or in conjunction of any malefic or other bad aspect to the malefics and these malefics themselves are afflicted, the quesited is in a poor condition and discontented.

If the ruler of the third is in the sixth, afflicted, the quesited is sick; if it separates from the ruler of the sixth, he has been ill. He is sick if the ruler of the sixth is in the third unless well situated.

In the seventh unafflicted, he is in the same country he went to and is well; if it is afflicted, then he has enemies and is disappointed in his contacts.

In the eighth he fears death and will die if the planet is in conjunction with the ruler of the eighth; if it is afflicted, he will die.

In the ninth, he has removed from where he first went or is forming some clerical engagements or is employed in traveling and intends being married there, if he is single. The ninth is the seventh from the third.

In the tenth in good aspect of the benefics, especially if the Sun rules the tenth, or in mutual reception with Jupiter or Venus, he is profitably employed; if combust and afflicted, there is danger of death.

In the eleventh, conjunction the ruler of the eleventh, he is among friends; a good aspect of the benefics shows him to be with friends and that he still wants to stay; but if the ruler of the third is afflicted by any of the malefics or is in his detriment or fall, then he is discontented and wishes to leave.

The ruler of the third in the twelfth and well aspected by the benefics and the benefics themselves unafflicted shows he will deal in merchandise by which he will gain; but if the ruler is afflicted in the twelfth, whether by aspects of the malefics or the ruler of the eighth, then he is discontented, troubled and not likely to see his home again.

Questions Regarding Agreements Between Brethren and Neighbors

If the ruler of the third is a benefic and in the first, third or ninth; the Moon in good aspect with a planet in the third or ninth or its ruler; the rulers of the first and third either in good aspect or mutual reception; Jupiter, Venus or the North Node well placed in the third or ninth, they will agree.

Those persons whose significators do not apply are most antagonistic and apt to disagree; but those whose significators apply are flexible, willing and yielding and desirous of agreement.

The agreement between the parties will not be agreeable if the rulers of the first and third or the first and the Moon are in bad aspect of each other; or if the South Node is in the third or in bad aspect of the ruler of the first; if there is any bad aspect of Uranus, Saturn or Mars to the Moon or ruler of the first, from the third or the first.

If the malefics are in the Ascendant, then the querent is stupid or to blame; but, if in the third, the quesited is the aggressive party. If Uranus, Saturn or Mars are retrograde, peregrine or combust, the malice and mischief they threaten will do more damage.

Is It Well to Go on a Short Journey?

The first, its ruler and the Moon are for the querent. The third and its ruler signify the journey.

In all travel questions pay particular attention to Mercury and Uranus as well as to the Moon. Mercury is a general travel planet; so is the Moon.

If the ruler of the third, first and Moon are direct, swift and well dignified or in conjunction, sextile or trine to each other; or if the Moon is in the third in sextile or trine to the first or its ruler; if the ruler of the third is in the third or ninth, sextile or trine, to the first or its ruler and if the ruler of the first is well dignified in the third—you are sure to go.

An Agreeable Journey

The ruler of the first or the Moon applying to a good aspect of a planet well placed in the third or ninth; the ruler of the third in good aspect to a fortunate planet in the first; Jupiter, Venus or the North Node in the third or ninth, a profitable journey, especially if the benefics apply by sextile or trine to the cusp of the first.

But if the ruler of the first is stationary, slow or retrograde, it shows hindrance and disappointment. Uranus, Neptune, Saturn, Mars or the South Node in the third, or afflicting the ruler of the third or the Moon, shows disappointment.

Uranus there denotes accidents and unexpected hindrances; Saturn there shows worry concerning such things as the house signifies of which Saturn is the ruler; Mars or the South Node in the third, danger of being robbed, and if in Aries, Leo or Sagittarius, accidents or lameness. Mars in the third is usually bad for journeys, even if it is well aspected.

If the ruler of the sixth afflicts the ruler of the first, third or Moon, or if the ruler of the sixth is with the South Node, he will be sick. If the ruler of the first, third or the Moon is afflicted by the South Node, Uranus, Saturn or Mars from angles; or if the ruler of the first or third are combust or badly aspected by the ruler of the eighth, especially if it is Uranus, Neptune, Saturn or Mars, there is danger of death.

The ruler of the twelfth afflicting the ruler of the third or first or the Moon shows he meets with private enemies; if the ruler of the seventh afflicts then he meets public enemies. The ruler of the twelfth shows slugs and sneak thieves, and the ruler of the seventh shows highwaymen.

Whatever planet afflicts the ruler of the third judge of the nature of the evil to be expected; and the house over which the planet rules will show the nature of the evil.

Of Anonymous Letters

Sometimes persons receive letters or telephone calls of a friendly, sometimes of an unfriendly nature, and the receiver knows not whence and from whom they come.

In order to discover the appearance and intention of the sender, take the third house and Mercury to denote the letter or message.

The ruler of the third describes the person. The house in which this ruler is placed indicates the relation or otherwise of the sender—as if in the first or in conjunction or good aspect with the ruler of the first, it is a person with whom the querent has frequent conversation. In the second, a person with whom the querent has had money transactions is indicated. And thus go around the chart and judge according to the signification of the twelve houses.

The ruler of the third in bad aspect with the ruler of the first, then the sender is malignant and ill disposed toward the querent. But if the ruler of the third is in its fall or detriment, the sender cannot hurt the querent; if powerful, judge the contrary.

Whether a Report Is True or False

This is judged by the ruler of the third house or planets in the third. The chart should be made for the exact time that the report was first heard.

The house occupied by the ruler of the third house cusp will show through which department of life the news will affect the questioner.

If there is a movable sign on the cusp of the Ascendant; if the Moon or Mercury, natural ruler of the third house, and the planet ruling the third cusp are in movable signs, it shows that the news will be contradicted.

But if a fixed sign rises or these planets are in fixed signs, it shows that the report is true and reliable.

If Mercury is severely afflicted, it shows the report to be false. The Moon angular in a fixed sign shows the report true.

Any planet in the third house conjunction the South Node, or the ruler of the third conjunction the South Node, indicates a false report with evil intentions.

The Moon in good aspect to Mercury shows that the report, if false, will be contradicted. A fixed sign on the cusp of the third house and a malefic retrograde in the third in this fixed sign, shows that it was a wicked report and may never be fully contradicted; if the Moon makes a good aspect to this planet, the report will not be so detrimental in its result.

If the planet is Neptune, it will be an exaggeration; if Uranus, it was maliciously invented through spite; if Saturn, it was intended to deceive for a selfish purpose; if Jupiter, it was more of a joke; if Mars, the person who told it is an enemy; if Venus, it was told through jealousy and if the Moon rules or is in the third, it is nasty gossip and spite.

Notice the aspect made between the ruler of the Ascendant and the ruler of the third. This will show what effect the news will have on the questioner. If the aspect is good, it will be a beneficial report, but if the aspect is evil, it will harm him.

Fourth House Questions

Questions about Property in General

The first house, its ruler, and the Moon denote the person who asks the question about property.

The seventh, its ruler, and planet in the seventh denotes the seller or person with whom he does business.

The fourth, its ruler, and planet in the fourth denotes the property.

The tenth, its ruler, and the planet in the tenth denotes the price of the property.

Will it Be Best for Me to Buy Property?

Yes, it will be, if any of the following rules apply: if Venus, Jupiter, the North Node, or the Part of Fortune is in the first and well aspected; if the ruler of the second is in the first or in good aspect to the ruler of the first; if the ruler of the second or the Moon is parallel or in good aspect to the fourth house cusp; if Venus or Jupiter or the North Node is in the fourth or in parallel or good aspect to the cusp of the fourth; if Saturn is well dignified by sign and aspect in the first or the fourth—this is favorable for purchasing property.

Will I Buy the Property?

You probably will if the ruler of the first or the Moon is in the fourth and well aspected or if the ruler of the fourth is in the first, well aspected; if the ruler of the first or the Moon is parallel, conjunct, sextile or trine the ruler of the fourth.

The parties will easily agree if the rulers of the first and seventh are well aspected to each other, especially if parallel or in mutual reception.

An agreement is indicated if the Moon translates the light between the ruler of the first and the ruler of the seventh, but if the ruler of the seventh applies to the ruler of the first by a square or opposition of mutual reception, the parties may agree but there will be hindrance and difficulty.

If the ruler of the first and ruler of the seventh do not aspect each other, but both these rulers make an aspect to a more powerful planet than themselves—this shows that the planet that collects the light of the good aspect of both these rulers will be the means of bringing them together for satisfactory agreements.

Mutual reception, collection and translation of light is a very powerful good aspect to bring questions of this nature to a satisfactory conclusion.

If the ruler of the seventh is in the seventh or makes any good aspect to Jupiter, Venus or the Part of Fortune, or if Jupiter or Venus is in the seventh, the seller will profit most.

Buying and Selling in General

The first house and its ruler denote the person who wishes to buy or sell.

The seventh and its ruler denote the person with whom we deal.

If a malefic is in the seventh, do not buy. If a malefic is in the first, there will be great labor and hindrance in the business contact, either way, and much trouble. If the Moon is void of course, there will be no bargain.

If the Moon separates from the malefics and applies to the benefics, you may buy; but if the Moon applies to the malefics, you could sell.

There must be some good aspect between the ruler of the first and the ruler of the seventh, such as translation or collection of light, for a business transaction.

These rules are practical and useful if applied right—someone loses and someone gains in all business transactions as long as it is based on the economic system of profit and loss.

There should be a planet disposing by sign of everything in the chart for the transaction to be profitable and to materialize.

The ruler of the seventh or ruler of the first or the Moon in its own sign shows profit and that the deal will probably materialize.

What Is the Quality and Value of the Property?

If Saturn, Neptune, Uranus, Mars, or the South Node is in the fourth afflicted or peregrine, the property will not be good.

If the ruler of the fourth is retrograde or in its detriment, the bargain is a bad one, and the property will not stay long with the buyer.

Jupiter, Venus or the North Node in the tenth shows that it is a good bargain, and, if it is income property, it will lease or rent well.

Uranus, Neptune, Saturn, Mars or the South Node in the tenth denotes the contrary, and if these planets are retrograde the owner will probably have trouble in collecting his rents, etc.

If there is no planet in the tenth, take the ruler of the sign on the cusp of the tenth and judge the results by the aspects it makes, good or bad.

Aries, Leo or Sagittarius on the fourth house cusp or the ruler of the fourth in one of these signs, judge that the property will be on a slope or hill and set back quite a way from the front of the property line, street or curbing. If it is land, it will be hard to cultivate.

Taurus, Virgo or Capricorn on the cusp of the fourth house or its ruler in any of these signs—if it is land, it will be of mixed soil and easily cultivated; very fertile.

Cancer, Scorpio or Pisces on the cusp of the fourth house or its ruler in any of these signs denotes that the land is wet, sometimes flooded, low, marshy, and probably has underground springs; in some cases oil, minerals, etc. are indicated.

Gemini, Libra or Aquarius on the cusp of the fourth or its ruler in any of these signs shows timber land; lots of shrubbery; probably high buildings.

A planet retrograde in the fourth house, especially Saturn, Neptune, Uranus or Mars shows it will prove a disappointment and loss to the buyer or owner. If Saturn, Uranus or Mars is retrograde in Scorpio, the land will be flooded.

If there are buildings on the property they will be in need of much repair. If these planets are in Pisces, the buildings will need new roofs, new paint, etc. Pluto or the above planets in Cancer shows peculiar conditions. Pluto especially is responsible for termite control and indicates dry rot.

Uranus, Saturn or Mars in Aries, Leo or Sagittarius shows the land to be barren and the property worthless, but Saturn in the above signs, especially in Sagittarius and well aspected, denotes the land could be cultivated by irrigation and probably grow timber or fruit-bearing trees.

Uranus, Neptune, Saturn or Mars retrograde in Gemini, Libra or Aquarius shows a bad bargain; the place would be old and in a run-down condition.

These planets retrograde in Taurus, Virgo or Capricorn denote very poor soil, cheap buildings, etc.—a bad bargain in general.

The price of property is judged by the tenth house sign and its ruler. If this ruler is angular, well dignified and aspected, the price will be high, but the property is probably worth it. The seller is hard to deal with.

If the ruler of the tenth is weak, cadent or badly aspected, the price will be cheap, and the seller in great need of money.

If Uranus, Neptune, Saturn, Mars or the South Node is in the seventh house and these planets do not rule the seventh cusp, be careful concerning contracts, agreements, etc., for this shows the seller will get the best of the bargain or will misrepresent the property.

Saturn retrograde in the seventh house in any question or even in a nativity shows the affairs of this house to be anything but fortunate.

A fortunate planet in the tenth house, well aspected and dignified, shows agreement and satisfaction to all parties concerned.

Questions About Moving

Do not move, stay where you are if it is possible, if you find the Moon, Jupiter, Venus, Mercury or the North Node in the first or fourth and unafflicted; if the ruler of the fourth and the first are in the seventh; if the ruler of the fourth and seventh are fortunate planets, swift or powerfully placed or if the ruler of the first is stronger than the ruler of the seventh.

Do not move if Uranus, Saturn or Mars is in the seventh or if evil planets are in the eighth house or afflicting the ruler of the eighth. It shows there would be trouble where the querent would go.

It would be best for the querent to move if the ruler of the seventh is making a parallel or good aspect to fortunate planets and if the rulers of the first and fourth are with malefics.

Uranus, Neptune, Saturn, Mars or the South Node, in the first or fourth, and if the ruler of the second is weak; Jupiter, Venus, Mercury or the North Node or Part of Fortune in the seventh and the ruler of the seventh stronger than the ruler of the first shows that it is best to move.

The Time the Querent Will Move

See when the ruler of the first or seventh or a planet in the seventh leaves the sign it is in when the question was asked, and this will show the time of the removal.

A movable sign on the cusp of the first and seventh shows a move or change. Planets changing signs indicate a change. The Moon in the last half of a sign, especially in a cardinal or common sign, indicates the same. Retrograde planets denote change when they turn direct.

The third house has to do with the present neighborhood; the ninth house, the future neighbors, providing the querent does move.

It will be well to consider the planet ruling the cusp of these houses and the last aspect, good or bad, which the Moon makes before it leaves the sign it is in when the question is asked. This shows what will transpire.

Will the Querent Inherit the Property?

The first, its ruler and the Moon signify the querent. The house and its ruler belonging to the person leaving the property by will or otherwise must be taken as his significator: as the fourth for the father; the tenth for mother, master or mistress; the third for brother, sister or cousin; the eleventh for a friend, etc.

The houses succeeding them denote the property, because they are their second houses, as the fifth for the father; the eleventh for the mother, master or mistress; the eighth for husband or wife; the fourth for sister, cousin, brother or neighbor; the twelfth for a friend, etc.

If the rulers of the querent and the other person's houses are in each other's reception by house, or applying by good aspect, the querent will inherit the expected property.

If the rulers of both their second houses are the same planet; or the ruler of the other person's second disposes of the querent's Part of Fortune in the natural first or second; or if the rulers of the querent's first and second dispose of the other person's ruler of the second, or the Part of Fortune; or if a benefic is in the second of the other person, in good aspect to the ruler of the first or Moon, or the querent's cusp or its ruler, or if there is translation of light between the ruler of the querent's second and the querent's respective rulers, all these are signs that the querent will inherit the property.

And if the ruler of the querent's second is combust or retrograde, the property will not do him much good; and if the ruler of the other person's second is so situated, there is not much property, if any.

If the two seconds' rulers apply to each other by evil aspect, provided there are other good testimonies that the property will be obtained, then it will be inherited but not without difficulty.

If there is separation from good aspects, it is to be feared the property will be left elsewhere, or that the querent's hopes will not materialize.

Of Treasures, Mines, Etc. Whether Recoverable or Not

To discover mines, hidden treasure, oil wells, mineral wells, and other things supposed to be concealed in the earth, you must observe whether there is any planet strong in the fourth, or if Jupiter or Venus is in the fourth; the rulers of the first and fourth joined in any of the angles; the Part of Fortune in the first or fourth, and the Sun and Moon or the benefics in good aspect; if so there is treasure.

Any planet dignified in fourth and in good aspect with the ruler of the seventh, then there is treasure; and if Saturn is ruler of the sixth, there is coal or other minerals and flowing substances.

Jupiter strong and ruler of the seventh, in good aspect of the ruler of the fourth, there is silver, etc., hidden; if Venus, women's ornaments; if Mercury, money, writings, medals, books, etc.; if the Sun, gold or jewels; if the Moon, silver and common articles; if Uranus, new invented articles.

There Is No Treasure, Etc.

If the Sun or Moon or the Part of Fortune is cadent, or make no aspect among themselves.

If Uranus, Saturn, or Mars is afflicted in the fourth, or Sun or Moon weak in the fourth.

The ruler of the fourth or Moon separating from good planets denotes there has been treasure hidden, but is removed. But if they separate from bad aspect, then say there never was treasure hidden.

Of Besieged Places

When it is required to be known whether a place besieged will be compelled to surrender, the fourth house must be the significator of the place besieged; the ruler of the fourth is the governor, commander, etc. and the fifth its means of defense in every respect.

If the ruler of the first is stronger than the ruler of the fourth, and joined with him in the first or tenth, or in reception with the Moon, or in its own house and disposing of the ruler of the fourth, ruler of the fourth combust, retrograde, or in no good aspect to a planet in the fourth, except to be well dignified in the fifth, it will be taken.

The ruler of the fourth in reception with the ruler of the first, the governor, commander, etc. is treacherous, and will surrender it.

If the ruler of the fourth is stronger than the ruler of the first, free from the malefics, supported by benefics, angular, in good aspect with Mars or the Sun, well dignified, or if the ruler of the Ascendant is unfortunate, afflicted, combust, retrograde, in the fourth, cadent or peregrine, it will not be taken.

Saturn in the first or tenth will defeat and disgrace the besiegers, and if in square or opposition to either the Sun or Moon, or to the ruler of the first, the commander of the expedition, or the querent, if he is one of the besiegers, will be killed or desperately wounded.

Places and Things Ruled by Signs and Planets

Aries—places where game is protected for purposes of sport. The retreat of thieves and outlaws, hilly ground, fresh plowed ground, laboratories, dentists' offices, distilleries, canneries, bakery shops, tool shops, barber shops, locksmiths, slaughter houses, smelters; rules ceilings, roofs, walls—outside and inside furnaces, chimneys.

Mars of Aries and Scorpio—red pepper, red wines, red garments; all sharp instruments, brass, war horses, war machinery, iron, steel; minerals; all sparkling and fiery substances; herbs—garlic, onions, hops, mustard. Mars rules the eagle, tiger, wolf and scorpion.

Taurus—after Aries plows and cultivates the ground, Taurus sows the seeds; rules wheat fields, gardens, trees near the house, pasture for cattle, places for storing furniture; banks, hotels, dark closets, trunks, dark places, low rooms.

Venus of Taurus and Libra—rules bedrooms, clothing, women's wearing apparel, rings, costume jewelry, dancing and dining rooms, theaters, perfume; herbs—peppermint, ferns, wheat, violet, rose; metals—copper, brass and bronze; minerals—all substances that reflect and take a high polish. Venus rules the dove, cat, rabbit, and swan.

Gemini—places where grain is stored, high places, schools, nurseries, all places for study purposes, garages, depots, mail boxes, libraries, tennis courts, badminton, attorneys' offices, stairways, upstairs rooms, the library, walls that are papered or decorated.

Mercury of Gemini and Virgo—rules bills, paper money, books, pictures, scientific instruments, pens, deeds, merchandise, messengers, and to some degree, publishers; metals—quick silver; minerals—all flowing and veined substances; herbs—carrots, parsley. Mercury rules the greyhound, bees, the fox, parrot, and dog.

Cancer—rules the sea, great rivers, lakes, springs, wells, cellars, cisterns, reservoirs, laundries, kitchens, sinks, hydrants.

Moon—rules the ocean, fountains, fish ponds, common sewers, all common commodities, poultry, silver plated articles, chinaware, kitchenware; metals—silver, aluminum; minerals—soft, smooth substances; herbs—melons, seaweed, lettuce, watercress, cauliflower.

Rules the turtle, owl, goose, and all kinds of shell fish and the goldfish.

Leo—places where wild beasts frequently come, woods, forests, jungles, deserts, parks, government buildings, castles, ballrooms, fireplaces, chimneys, dens in homes, places of amusement.

Sun rules theaters, splendid apartments, gold things, valuable articles, yellow apparel; metals—gold; minerals—all glistening substances to which light seems intrinsic; herbs—rice, honey, poppy, sunflower, orange; Leo rules the lion and peacock.

Virgo—studies, studios, bookcases, closets, dairies, cornfields, hay racks, malt houses, storehouses for groceries, secret compartments, cabinets, chicken ranches.

Libra—rules outhouses, sawmills, inner chambers, upstairs bedrooms, attics, wardrobes, mountain tops or high on hilltops where the air is fresh and cool.

Scorpio—rules vaults, sewers, places where insects breed, sinks, toilets, dirty places, marshes, vineyards, stagnant pools and places with bad odors in general, cesspools, medicine cabinets.

Sagittarius—rules stables for horses, fireplaces in upper rooms, army barracks, stores for ammunition, high sloping ground.

Jupiter rules churches, altars, courts of justice, wardrobes, neat and curious places, woods, orchards, bushes, man-tailored clothes, wool merchandise, horses and all domestic fowls, private garages; metals—tin; minerals—common and useful substances; herbs—honey, oil, fruits, asparagus, sage, cloves, rhubarb, dandelion, mints; rules the elephant and whale.

Capricorn—rules churchyards, cemeteries, crematories, tombs, urns, places where lumber is stored, bushy places, dark places or corners near the ground or threshold in low houses, prisons, snow sheds, city hall, chamber of commerce, main business district.

Saturn rules deserts, woods, dirty places in the home, land owners, dark-colored wool garments, all agricultural implements, wooden things, glue, gravel, leather articles, sand; metal—lead;

minerals—dull, heavy substances and drosses; herbs—barley, bran, parsnips, spinach, holly. Rules the mule and donkey.

Aquarius—all places recently dug up, places used for airplanes and aeronautic apparatus, electric lighting systems, roofs and eves of buildings, upstairs rooms, artistic things on the wall, shelves, hangers for clothing.

Uranus—rules railways, steam engines, gas tanks, asylums, infirmaries, railway stations, workhouses, places of confinement, heavy machinery, old coins, antiques, explosives, electric devices, radio sets, television, X-ray; metals—uranium, radium; minerals—electric and magnetic substances; herbs—probably the same as for Venus and the Moon. Uranus is probably responsible for the grafting of certain fruit trees and flowers.

Pisces—places where waterfowl, fishes and water plants are found, bathing places, watermills, beaches, old hermitages, mossy places, fisheries, fish canneries, places where fluids or medicines are kept.

Neptune rules hospitals, charities, bogus companies, secret and mysterious places. Has much to do with motion pictures, especially photography. Rules mediums, profits, deep-sea divers, submarines, aquariums, mistletoe and orchids.

Of Things Mislaid or Hidden: Where to Find Them

If the thing hidden or mislaid belongs to the one who asks the question, always take the second house and its ruler. Refer to Theft Questions.

It is not well to answer a question of this nature for anyone except the person who has lost or mislaid the article.

If the ruler of the second is in any of the four angles, it is in the home, especially if the Part of Fortune or the dispositor of the Part of Fortune is in any of the angles and either of these makes a good aspect to the ruler of the second house from angles.

If the Moon is in the second in good aspect to the ruler of the first; the Moon in the tenth in good aspect to the ruler of the tenth or to the ruler of the first; the ruler of the first in the second; the Sun and Moon are trine to each other or to the cusp of the second; if the ruler of the second is in the eleventh or fourth; the ruler of the eighth in the first or in good aspect to the ruler of the first; if Jupiter, Venus or the North Node is in the eleventh or second; if the ruler of the fourth is in good aspect to the ruler of the first or second; the ruler of the fourth in the fourth and well dignified; the ruler of the first and fourth the same planet.

All this shows that the article or thing will be found again and that it is merely misplaced.

If the Sun and Moon are under the earth, that is from the first to the sixth house, even if they are well aspected, there is not much hope of finding the lost article.

If the ruler of the second is severely afflicted and makes no aspect to the Ascendant, it will never be found unless the Moon or a fast moving planet translates the light between these rulers.

If the ruler is going out of one sign into another, the article is behind something or has fallen between two rooms or places, such as between the wainscoting or between niches or boards at the joining of two rooms, or in compartments of cabinets, safe, drawer, etc.

If the ruler of the second is in the Ascendant, the article is in that part of the home where the querent is in the habit of staying, but if the ruler of the second is in the tenth, it is in the hall or dining room; if the querent is a mechanic or tradesman, it is in his shop.

Example Charts

The two charts included here are authentic and given as examples to show how the rules given in this book should be used. These rules apply satisfactorily in answering questions of this nature in minute detail.

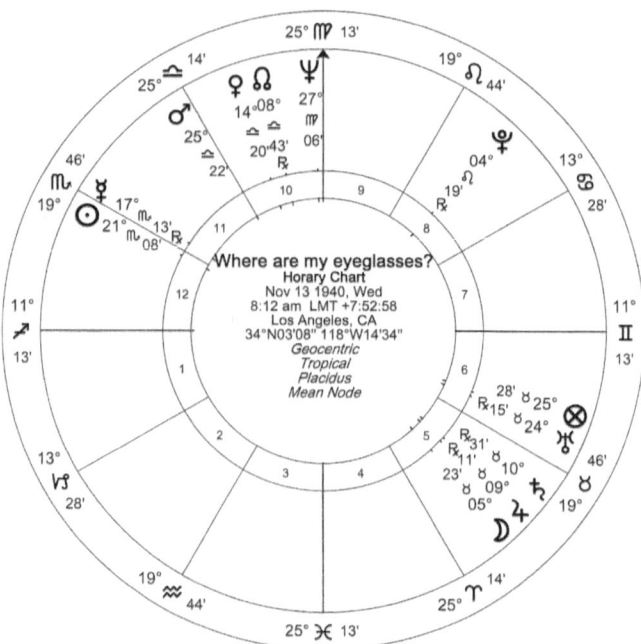

The question, "Where are my eyeglasses?" was asked by a woman, November 13, 1940 at 8:12 a.m. True Local Mean Time, at Los Angeles, on a Mercury Day and in a Saturn Hour.

The sign Sagittarius on the eastern horizon represents the querent; Jupiter is her ruler and the Moon co-ruler. The sign on the second cusp, Saturn the ruler, denotes the lost eyeglasses.

Let us apply the rules for answering any question of this nature.

If the ruler or co-ruler of the thing inquired about, or the Part of Fortune or its dispositor is in any of the angles of the chart when the question is asked or if the ruler or co-ruler of the lost article are in conjunction, the lost article is in the home of the one who asked the question.

Another rule says it is in the home if the ruler of the querent and the ruler of the fourth cusp is the same planet.

Horary Questions by House

Now, Saturn, ruler of the eyeglasses, is not in any of the angles. Neither is the co-ruler, the Moon, or the Part of Fortune, but the disposer of the Moon, Saturn and the Part of Fortune, the planet Venus, is in the tenth house.

The Moon, co-ruler, and Saturn are conjunct.

The planet Jupiter rules the querent, and it also rules the fourth house cusp.

We now have three reasons to say definitely that the glasses are in her home. Venus, the disposer of the three chief significators in the sign Taurus, is in its own sign, Libra, in the tenth house; this signifies they are in her home.

Now we must find out where in the home the article is to be found. Venus will to some extent show the location.

Referring to our rules, we find that Venus signifies bedrooms, wardrobes, and woman's apparel.

Libra denotes closets and guest chambers. An air sign, Libra also describes things either hanging up on something or on a shelf, things above the floor or in upstairs rooms.

Going back to the lost article signified by Saturn and the Moon, co-ruler, we find them in the earth sign Taurus.

Taurus rules dark places and closets; Saturn rules dark places; Jupiter, Moon, and Saturn conjunct in Taurus denote merchandise.

Synthesizing the above, I could safely say the glasses could be found in the pocket (dark place) of a tailored suit (Jupiter, Saturn and the Moon in Taurus) in a closet (Taurus) in the northwest bedroom (Libra is west and Pisces on the fourth cusp, her home, is north by west—the fourth house is north).

I advised the woman to look in the pocket of a tailored suit she had recently worn and she would find her glasses.

The reason for my saying a "suit she had recently worn" was because of the woman's ruler, Jupiter, and Saturn, ruler of the

Horary Astrology

glasses, and Moon co-ruler being in such close aspect in the same sign.

Venus, ruling women's wearing apparel, is not with this satellitium, showing that she had more than one suit and lots of clothes. Libra denotes upstairs bedrooms.

These planets together in the same sign and in such close aspect showed but a short separation between the woman and her glasses. This caused me to say "the suit she had last worn."

Now we will apply the rules for the translation of light.

The Moon, co-ruler of the woman and her glasses, translates the light from Jupiter, ruler of Sagittarius (the woman), to the conjunction of Saturn, ruler of the glasses, and makes this conjunction on the same day the question was asked. This shows she could find her glasses the same day.

The woman did as instructed and found her glasses in the pocket of a tailored suit she had worn the night before to the theater (note the planet in the fifth house of pleasure).

She said she never remembered putting them in her pocket and had never done so before. She was curious to know how I could tell her which suit to search as she had three tailored suits, and how I could say it was in an upstairs bedroom and the northwest one as there were four bedrooms upstairs.

I explained to her how it was possible through a horary chart to answer any question in detail.

She would have eventually found them because Jupiter, Moon and Saturn were in Taurus (possessions), but these planets in a fixed sign in a succedent house and with Jupiter, Saturn, Uranus and Mercury retrograde, it could have taken some time. She admitted she had made quite a search before asking the question.

The Sun above the earth, coming to the sextile of Neptune, co-ruler of the fourth house cusp, and Neptune in the tenth house, shows recovery.

But the Moon translating the light from Jupiter (the woman) to Saturn (the glasses) ruled my decision from the moment I put up the chart.

It was interesting and more than gratifying to prove all the rest of the chart in detail.

This proves how necessary it is to follow the rules given for every question that we are asked to read. We will answer questions accurately and successfully if we do.

The question, "Where is my money?" was asked by a woman on September 11, 1940 at 8:45 a.m. True Local Mean Time, at Los Angeles, on a Mercury Day and a Mars Hour.

This chart shows an entirely different and rather difficult reading as to house position.

The question was asked by one woman about another woman who had lost some money. The chart was set for the time the woman, represented by Libra on the eastern horizon, first heard the other woman, represented by the seventh house sign, Aries, say she had lost some money.

But the woman who lost the money did not ask the question.

Therefore, in all questions of this nature we take the first house for the querent and the seventh house for the quesited, making the seventh house the first house for this question or to represent the woman who lost the money.

The eighth house becomes the other woman's second or the lost money.

Referring to our rules we find that if the ruler of the second is in any of the angles the article is in the home.

Venus rules Taurus on the eighth house cusp, which in this question is the other woman's second or money house.

Venus is in her fourth house, counting the tenth as the other woman's fourth, in the fixed sign Leo and conjunction Pluto.

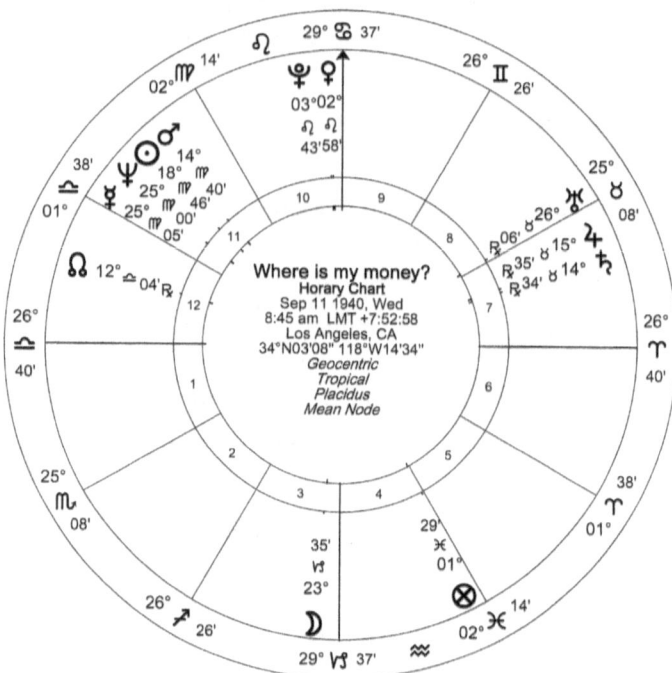

Again applying our rule, if the dispositor of the Part of Fortune or the Part of Fortune is in any angle, it is in the home.

The Part of Fortune is in the woman's tenth house, counting the fourth of this chart as her tenth, and Jupiter, the disposer of the Part of Fortune, is in the woman's first house in Taurus, and it is retrograde. Again, we have enough proof to say that the money is in the woman's home.

To find out where in the home the money is located we will look first to Venus, ruler of her money, because it rules Taurus, the sign on her second house cusp and is in the fourth.

Our rules say this indicates it is in the home, probably where an older person, father or mother, stays; Venus is a feminine planet, so we could say it represents the woman's mother. Also, ruler of second in fourth.

Venus in a fixed sign would signify the mother was fixed in her home (not visiting).

The Sun, ruler of Leo, intercepted in the fourth house, rules valuables and in this question, money.

The Sun must therefore be given particular attention.

The Sun is in the woman's fifth house in the scientific and serving sign Virgo, and Mercury, the ruler of Virgo, is in this house in its own sign; it therefore disposes of everything in the chart.

Mercury is especially important in a question of this kind as Mercury rules paper money or bills; in this case the money lost was paper bills.

In considering the above, Mercury in Virgo will show where the bills are.

Mercury in its own dual sign, Virgo, with Neptune, the Sun and Mars shows more than one bill.

The Moon co-ruler makes three aspects; and Mercury parallel Neptune and trine Uranus shows two or three bills.

Mercury in the same sign with the Sun shows they are valuable.

Venus, the Moon, Mercury and Uranus all have to do with this woman's money and therefore will answer this particular question.

The Moon, because it is co-ruler and ruler of Cancer on the woman's fourth house cusp (again a clue to the woman's mother); Venus, because it rules the woman's second house cusp (her money); Mercury, because it is the natural ruler of paper bills and disposes of everything in this chart; and Uranus, because it is in the woman's money house—all must be considered.

First, because Venus disposes of Uranus and rules the woman's money house, we will start with Venus in Leo intercepted in the fourth house (her home).

Venus in Leo in the fourth would describe a place near a wall or on a shelf.

The Moon, co-ruler of the woman and her money and ruler of Cancer on the fourth house cusp, is in the earth sign Capricorn, describing dark wood.

Mercury in the earth sign Virgo describes merchandise and scientific things, and, since it is in the fifth house, something to do with pleasure.

Uranus in this question rules modern or antique things, as well as all uncommon novelties. Venus conjunction Pluto in Leo, the sign of pleasure, confirms this.

The majority of planets in earth signs signifies a place near the ground or very close to the floor in a dark place.

The Moon in Capricorn rules wooden things, the Part of Fortune in Pisces shows that it is hidden, Mercury in Virgo and parallel the planet Neptune, ruler of Pisces, in the fifth house in the scientific and domestic sign Virgo, shows it is concealed.

Leo, Cancer and Virgo, because of their close relation in this question, describe a living room that could be used as a combination dining room and sleeping quarters (or where the mother would sleep).

Using all the above analysis for confirmation, the woman was told to go to the southeast corner of the living room (the sign Virgo is south, and Leo, intercepted in the fourth house, is east by north; Cancer on the fourth cusp is north, and Venus in Leo is east by north and Virgo is south) in her radio.

Venus conjunction Pluto in Leo, pleasure, and Mercury in Virgo, scientific instruments) indicates that it was probably between the wall or at the side of a drawer or niche or between boards.

Moon in Capricorn rules wood and the Moon just leaving the sign shows it has fallen between something; Mercury, ruler of paper bills, leaving the sign, also shows it has fallen behind or between wood. She would find her money.

Still, she did not find it. Mars, ruler of the woman who lost the money, is in the fifth house in Virgo; this shows she is with or has had something to do with the money recently, but neither the Moon, co-ruler, or Mercury (bills) or Venus (money) aspect Mars, ruler of the woman.

The Moon, co-ruler, does translate the light from a trine aspect of Mercury (the money) and Neptune to Uranus in the woman's second house in Taurus, the money sign; this shows the woman would get her money through someone else, the mother, because the Moon rules Cancer and the mother.

Now let us consider the collection of light aspect. Venus, ruler of the second house cusp (the woman's money), and Mars, ruler of the woman who lost or misplaced the money, are not aspecting each other, but both are in aspect to a heavier planet.

Mars is in trine aspect to Jupiter and Uranus in the sign Taurus.

Venus, ruler of Taurus and the woman's money, will square Jupiter.

These translation and collection of light aspects show she will recover her money through another person, in this case, the mother. This is exactly what happened.

When the woman could not find the money, the mother, who believed so much in my being able to say she was in the home and that the radio did sit in the corner designated, took a flashlight and nail file and dug behind a shelf at the bottom of the radio, close to the floor, and found the bills, which had slipped behind the boards of this shelf; and there were three bills.

But the mother did not search for nor find this money until the morning of September 13, or three days after the chart was set up and delineated.

The Moon is three degrees from a trine to Uranus, the last aspect it makes before leaving the sign.

Mercury, ruler of paper bills, moved to Libra on the 13th. This definitely proves the time element.

The Moon in a cardinal sign, Mercury in a mutable sign, the Moon decreasing slows the time.

Retrograde planets give delay; the Mercury day denotes uncertainty, but is considered good for money matters, especially in this instance when paper money was involved; the Moon trine Uranus shows gain.

The Mars hour is energetic and gives much confidence in the matter, but it is well to have a thorough understanding of any matter to be attended to on a Mars hour.

This no doubt shows why the mother kept searching after the woman did not find her money.

Retrograde planets in the woman's first and second houses shows she was careless or could not be bothered.

Retrograde planets and the decreasing Moon show delay, but the common and fixed signs mean success after a reasonable time.

This is a chart proving to us the importance of always considering translation and collection of light as a definite, favorable answer for certain questions to be brought to perfection, and if we had not used them in this question, we probably would say, since Uranus is in a fixed sign and retrograde in the woman's second house, Mars (ruler of the woman) and Venus (ruler of her money) make no aspect to each other, and Mars applying to a trine aspect of a retrograde planet in her money house—that she would be disappointed in regaining her money.

But when we use our rules according to instruction, we may answer with success, and be certain of the definite outcome of any question. Again I suggest that the astrologer give translation and collection of light aspects much attention.

Fifth House Questions

Lotteries, prizes, prize money, raffles, games, cards, horse races, football, purchasing of amusement shares, winning a bet or wager.

If it is a personal question, take the rising sign and its ruler to denote the person who asks the question; the fifth house, its ruler, and any planet in the fifth to denote the gain or loss; the seventh house to show the opponent or whoever we contact in such matters.

The rules for winning are as follows:

The rulers of the first and fifth or first and second in the tenth house and the Moon making a parallel or any good aspect to either of these rulers is a sure sign of gain for the querent.

Venus, Jupiter, or the Part of Fortune in the first, Venus or Jupiter ruling the first, second or fifth or in either of these houses and not afflicted by the malefics or retrograde shows definite gain.

The Moon parallel or in any good aspect to the ruler of the first or second or in good aspect or conjunction to the Part of Fortune; the Part of Fortune in the first, fifth, tenth or fourth and not badly afflicted by the malefics or by the ruler of the first, fifth or seventh shows gain for the querent.

If the ruler of the first is parallel, conjunct or in any good aspect to the ruler of the fifth, especially in mutual reception, or the ruler of the first a benefic and in the tenth or first; the ruler of the fifth stronger than the ruler of the seventh; the ruler of the fifth separating from any good aspect of the ruler of the seventh or eighth and immediately applies to a parallel or good aspect to the ruler of the first or second.

The Moon translating the light from the ruler of the fifth to the ruler of the second; the majority of planets angular—all of these are testimonies for gain. The North Node in the first, second, fifth or tenth is a weak testimony for gain.

The testimonies of loss follow:

If the ruler of the fifth, second or seventh is a malefic planet and in its detriment or fall, retrograde or Via combust; the ruler of the first, fifth or the Moon afflicted in cadent houses; the ruler of the fifth in the seventh in good aspect or mutual reception with the ruler of the seventh. The ruler of the fifth separating from the ruler of the first or second and applying to a parallel or other good aspect to the ruler of the seventh, eighth, or to Uranus, Saturn, Mars or the South Node, you may expect to lose.

The Part of Fortune in the seventh, the ruler of the seventh in good aspect to the Part of Fortune or to the ruler of the eighth.

Uranus, Saturn or Mars in the fifth and not the ruler of the sign on the cusp of the fifth, the South Node in the first, fifth or twelfth house denote disappointment through such matters.

If you find equal testimonies, then judge in favor of the most powerful ruler to win and be sure to use the Table for the Debilities and Dignities of Planets to successfully answer questions of this nature and decide in favor of the greatest number of reasons or testimonies.

Information Regarding Football Games, Etc.

Any chart erected for such matters is either an event or an inception.

Events like football or baseball are called inceptions because they happen periodically.

The following rules are to be used in the judgment of games.

In the first place, there seems to be much confusion and uncertainty as to house position for the teams.

I use the Ascendant and its ruler for the home team wherever the game is played, and the fifth house, its ruler, and planets in the fifth for the game. The seventh house and its ruler are for the visiting team.

The eleventh house is the fifth from the seventh or the game of the visiting team. The Moon is co-ruler for both teams. These are simple horary rules.

Set up a chart for the time and place the game will be played.

The football season lasts about four months, and the duration of the game is about two hours.

Those of us living in Los Angeles are naturally interested in the University of Southern California and the University of California.

The sign Aquarius is rising at the beginning of the football season in the chart erected for Los Angeles, so at 4:00 p.m. the sign Pisces would be on the eastern horizon. I judge the finish of the game by turning the wheel from Aquarius to Pisces to see where the planets will be at that time and what aspect the Moon will be making. Apply these rules for other teams in other cities.

The home team will win if the rulers of the first and fifth or the Moon is rising toward the Midheaven, provided these rulers are not afflicted, retrograde, or combust.

The ruler of the fifth (the game) in the fifth, dignified, and better aspected to the ruler of the first than to the ruler of the seventh; a planet in its own sign in the fifth; the Moon making a better aspect to the ruler of the first or fifth than to the ruler of the seventh or eleventh; the Part of Fortune in the first, second or fifth; and angular planets are sure signs of gain, provided these planets are not in any way afflicted.

The Part of Fortune in the seventh or in the seventh house sign or in the eighth or eleventh indicates gain for the visiting team.

The ruler of the eleventh in the eleventh shows the same.

The Moon better aspected to the ruler of the seventh and eleventh than to the ruler of the first and fifth; the ruler of the seventh a benefic and on the angle, even though it is retrograde, is more powerful than the ruler of the first if that ruler is retrograde or combust and shows gain for the visiting team.

The Moon translating the light from either the ruler of the first or seventh to the ruler of the fifth or eleventh or to planets in either of these houses shows gain for that team.

The ruler of the fifth separating from the ruler of the seventh and applying to the ruler of the first indicates gain for the home team.

If the Moon is badly aspected or the ruler of the fifth is afflicted, or if the planets in the fifth are malefics, retrograde or combust, this indicates some of the players may be hurt.

If the Moon afflicts Mercury, the game may be slow but full of spectacular plays.

If the Moon is void of course or making only one or two aspects, the score may be small or tied depending on the house position of the Moon at the end of the game.

The score of any game is difficult and uncertain to judge, and I would say it cannot be successfully ascertained. But I have noticed if the Moon makes many aspects, and especially if it is in its own sign, the scores will be large.

An increasing and decreasing Moon makes much difference, and, since the planet Pluto has entered the natural fifth house sign of Leo, all scores have been phenomenal.

If, at the beginning of any game the Part of Fortune is in the second or fifth house, it will be in the first or fourth house when the wheel is turned for the end of the game.

If it is in the eighth or eleventh house at the beginning, it will then be in the seventh or tenth at the end of the game.

I always use the Table of Dignities and Debilities of the planets in working with football games and judge accordingly.

Like anything else of a speculative or sporting nature, football games are difficult to judge correctly, but can be successfully worked out if we have enough charts, stay with the rules, and consider the dignities and debilities the planets may enjoy or suffer and the fixed stars.

However, astrology is not and should not be used for gambling or betting purposes, and I advise the student not to expect satisfaction if he uses the wheel for the time the game begins as a horary question.

This is the horary (hour) of an inception of a periodical event and should be judged that way.

Whether a Woman Will Have Children

Consider the first house for the woman and the fifth house for her children.

If the ruler of the first is in the fifth or the ruler of the fifth, or the Moon is in the first house and well aspected, she will probably have children.

See if the ruler of the first is conjunct Venus, Jupiter or the Moon in the fifth, or if a fortunate planet is in the first, third, fifth, ninth, or eleventh houses; if they are, this indicates that she may have children.

Cancer, Scorpio or Pisces on the cusp of the fifth house, or the ruler of the first or fifth or the Moon in these signs, or the Moon translating the light between the ruler of the first and fifth, indicates that she will have children.

The Sun should always be considered in a question of this nature, as the Sun is the natural ruler of the fifth house.

To Find How Many Children a Woman Will Have

It is advisable to use the natal chart for this question; however, it is possible to tell from the question, by the number of good aspects between the ruler of the fifth house and the benefics, how many she may have.

Venus, Jupiter, the Moon, or the ruler of the first in the fifth in

Cancer or Scorpio gives more than one child.

Pisces on the cusp of the fifth, and the Moon conjunction Venus in Pisces, gives three or more children depending on the number of aspects made.

The parallels and conjunctions are said to give large families, trines more than three, sextiles two or more. The signs Gemini and Virgo and Leo are not considered fruitful signs.

When these signs occupy the cusps of the first and fifth, and the planets Venus, Sun, or Mercury are in bad aspect to Saturn, Uranus, or Mars or the South Node or the Moon, or when any of these malefics occupy the fifth house, children are usually denied; also if the ruler of the fifth afflicts any of the above planets, children are denied.

If a child should be born under these influences, it will not live long, or it may be severely afflicted, physically or mentally.

A Woman Asks if She Is With Child

She is, if the ruler of the first or the Moon is applying to the ruler of the fifth by conjunction, parallel, sextile or trine; or if the ruler of the first or the Moon is in the fifth; if the ruler of the fifth is with its dispositor; also if the rulers of the fifth and first are in fruitful signs in the fifth, seventh or eleventh houses; the planets Jupiter or Venus in the angles, swift and free from affliction.

If the Moon is in the seventh house and the ruler of the seventh house is in the eleventh; if the Moon is making a good aspect to the ruler of the eleventh or if the Moon is in the eleventh and making a good aspect to the ruler of the seventh in the seventh.

The ruler of the first, fifth or the Moon in mutual reception with a planet in an angular house. This all indicates that the woman is with child.

But if you find the ruler of the first and the ruler of the fifth afflicted in the signs Gemini, Leo, Virgo, or the malefic planets in the fifth and retrograde, the South Node or the Moon in the fifth, the Moon afflicting Venus, she is either not with child or will miscarry.

Will the Child Be a Boy or Girl

It will be a boy if Aries, Gemini, Leo, Libra, Sagittarius, or Aquarius occupy the cusp of the fifth house; or if the rulers of the first and fifth are in any of these signs; or the dispositor of the Moon in any of the above signs.

If the ruler of the first is Uranus, Saturn, Jupiter, Mars or the Sun, and the ruler of the fifth is Venus or Jupiter, take the strongest testimony by the Moon's aspects to masculine signs; this gives a boy.

If the foregoing testimonies are in feminine signs, the child will be a girl.

The planet Mercury is dual and convertible and can represent either sex.

Observe Mercury closely and see what sign it occupies and to which planet it applies.

Suppose, for example, the sign Virgo was on the cusp of the natal fifth house, and the planet Mercury was in a feminine sign, applying by a close aspect to the planet Jupiter in a masculine sign; this would indicate a boy if the child should live.

However this would be only one indication of the child's sex, and we must always have three definite reasons to make any question radical or to answer any question successfully.

This is the chart of a question asked by an expectant mother who wanted to know whether the child would be a boy or girl. The question was asked June 5, 1940 at 9:18 a.m. Local Time, on a Mercury day and a Mars hour.

The masculine sign Leo on the cusp of the first house, ruled by a masculine planet, the Sun, represents the querent (the expectant

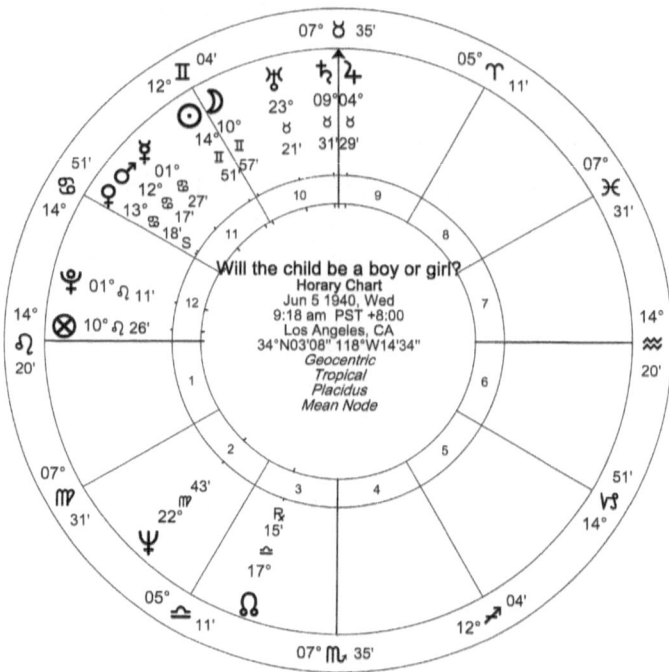

mother) and shows she might be partial to a baby boy.

The fifth house is read for the expected child (boy or girl). Applying our rules for a question of this nature, a boy is indicated by the sign Sagittarius occupying the cusp of the fifth house.

Sagittarius is a masculine sign and Jupiter, its ruler, is a masculine planet, but Jupiter is in a feminine sign. The Sun, natural fifth house ruler, is in a masculine sign, Gemini.

But we find a dual sign on the cusp of the fifth house and the majority of planets in feminine signs and the Sun, natural fifth house ruler in a dual sign—does this signify twins?

The Moon, co-ruler of the question, is applying to a conjunction of the Sun, a masculine planet. Moreover, Mercury is dual and convertible and can represent either sex. Mercury has just left the conjunction of the Sun, a masculine planet.

The Moon, co-ruler of the question, is conjunct the Sun, and the Moon and Mercury are in mutual reception. This makes Mercury have a masculine vibration; the child would be a boy.

The woman was uncertain of her time, but we decided that the child would be born around the middle of December.

One of the rules says to count from the fifth house sign to see how long it will be before confinement. Jupiter, ruler of the fifth cusp, is six signs from the fifth house, counting Sagittarius as the first house of the child; so it would be about six months.

Also, if the planet Saturn is the ruler of the seventh cusp, she has had quickening.

However, Jupiter, ruler of the fifth, is not quite conjunct Saturn—it lacks about five degrees—and the Moon is not quite conjunct the Sun; this shows she is almost ready for the quickening.

We also decided that the birth would be either a forced delivery or a caesarian birth because the last aspect the Moon makes is a square aspect to Neptune.

Neptune is ruler of the eighth house cusp, which is the fourth house from the fifth, the child's first house, and the Moon co-ruler is four signs from Neptune.

The Sun, natural fifth house ruler (children), is four signs from Neptune and in a square aspect.

But the child would live as the planet Venus, ruler of the tenth house cusp, the sixth house from the fifth or the child's health house, is sextile Neptune; also, the Sun and Moon are sextile the Part of Fortune, and Mars, ruler of Scorpio on the fourth house cusp—the end of the matter for the woman—is sextile Neptune. The Moon and Mercury in mutual reception show the birth of life.

The baby was a boy born December 17, 1940. It was a Mercury day and a Mars hour when the question was asked; Mercury had just left the conjunction of the Sun and was moving to a sextile of Jupiter and Saturn and a conjunction of Mars.

Both Mars and Mercury were coming to a sextile of the planet Neptune, ruler of the eighth house and the baby's fourth house (as the eighth is the fourth from the fifth); there would be plenty of opportunity for the baby to be born and to live and so it did.

We gave the birth date as December 15, and the child was born December 17.

Will There Be Twins?

Gemini, Sagittarius and Pisces are called dual signs and if any one of these occupies the first or fifth house and Jupiter, Venus, the Sun or the Moon is in these signs, it usually gives twins.

Also, if the ruler of the first and the ruler of the fifth are in these signs, twins are indicated. But unless all these occur it is not safe to predict twins.

Fixed or movable signs on the first and fifth cusps, and the Sun and Moon in either of these houses usually gives one child.

Length of Time a Woman Has Been Pregnant

Consider the rulers of the first and fifth and the Moon. If you find the dispositor of the Moon angular and the Moon separating from a conjunction or sextile of the ruler of the first, she has either just conceived or is in the first month of pregnancy; if from a trine, the third or fifth month is indicated; if from a square, her fourth month is shown; if from an opposition, her seventh month is shown.

If Saturn is in the seventh or ruler of the seventh, this usually shows she is quickened.

Time of Birth

Birth usually occurs when the Sun or Mars is conjunct the ruler of the first or fifth or when the ruler of the fifth is in the fifth.

Observe the time when the ruler of the first either transits the place of the Moon, Jupiter or Venus, especially in the first, fifth or eleventh houses.

See how far the ruler of the fifth is from the fifth house, and allow one month for every sign.

Also see how far the ruler of the fifth is from the ruler of the first. Some astrologers say that if Saturn is in the seventh house or ruler of that cusp, and the ruler of the fifth or the Moon is separating from Saturn or the Moon is separating from the ruler of the fifth, the woman is quickened.

This is a difficult question to answer, and I do not think it can be predicted without years of practice and much experience.

I advise the astrologer not to answer a question of this nature for anyone except the expectant mother.

Whether a Child Will Live or Die

Take the fifth house for a first child.

If the ruler of the fifth is retrograde, or combust the Sun, or in the third, sixth, ninth or twelfth houses, or if this ruler is in its detriment or fall, weak or afflicted by the rulers of the eighth or twelfth or in these houses and afflicted, the child will not live.

The ruler of the first and fifth afflicting each other; Saturn, Uranus, Mars retrograde in the fifth or the South Node or the Moon in the fifth—all indicate that the child may die in infancy.

Here is a rule worth considering: if the ruler of the sign on the cusp of the fifth house is afflicted by the ruler of the sign on the cusp of the eighth house, there will be much sorrow and loss in affairs and matters represented by the fifth and eighth houses.

About Lost or Runaway Children

The ruler of the sign on the cusp of the first house and the Moon denote the father and mother of the child inquired about.

The fifth house denotes the first child. This house becomes the first house of the question, the ruler of the fifth and Mercury, the child's significators.

The child returns or is found if the ruler of the fifth or Mercury is retrograde, or if the ruler of the fifth or a planet in the fifth or Mercury is applying to a good aspect of the ruler of the first or to a planet in the Ascendant.

The Moon translating the light from Mercury or from the ruler of the fifth house cusp to the ruler of the first indicates that news will be received of the child.

If the Moon translates the light from the ruler of the first to the ruler of the fifth, news of the child will also be received.

If Mercury is in the fifth house or ruler of the fifth house sign and combust the Sun, the child is in a serious condition.

If the ruler of the fifth or the Moon or Mercury is afflicted by Saturn, Uranus, Mars or the South Node, it shows that the child's condition is sorrowful.

The child may never return or be found if the ruler of the fifth is in the third, seventh or ninth houses, or if the rulers of the first and fifth are square, opposition, or separating from any aspect to each other.

Of a Messenger Sent on Important Business

The first house and its ruler denote the sender; the ruler of the fifth, the messenger; the Moon is the message; and the seventh and its ruler, the person and place to whom it is sent.

When the ruler of the fifth house separates from the ruler of the seventh and applies to a good aspect of the ruler of the first, the messenger has succeeded.

If he separates from the ruler of the second or eighth by any aspect, he brings money with him.

If the Moon separates from benefics, the business has succeeded well, but, if from malefics, not very well.

If the ruler of the fifth or Mercury translates the light of the ruler of the seventh to the ruler of the first, he has succeeded.

What Takes Place on the Journey

A benefic in the third or ninth denotes traveling, but a malefic there shows the contrary.

Saturn causes privations and disappointments.

Mars or the South Node, danger of robbers, losses, and slander.

Where there is reason to apprehend danger, the ruler of the fifth in opposition to a malefic or either the Sun or Moon in the same situation, is a very bad symbol.

If the Moon alone be afflicted, the messenger meets with bad reception. If slow, there will be delay.

If the ruler of the fifth applies to Uranus, Neptune, Saturn or Mars by square or opposition before he can separate from the ruler of the seventh, it denotes impediment to the party to whom it was sent.

But if the ruler of the fifth makes a square or opposition of the malefics after he has separated from the ruler of the seventh, he will receive disappointments on his way home.

The Time of the Messenger's Return Home

The return is indicated when the ruler of the fifth comes to a sextile, trine or conjunction of the ruler of the first.

When the Moon separates from the ruler of the fifth and applies to the ruler of the first, the querent will have word of his messenger.

The application of the significator to a ponderous planet denotes the day he will hear of the messenger.

The ruler of the fifth retrograde indicates that he will return when the planet goes direct or according to the number of degrees until it turns direct.

The Character of the Messenger

Consider the ruler of the fifth, what planet he is, and whether he is dignified or weak.

If the rulers of the fifth and first houses are in mutual reception or in good aspect from good houses, the messenger is faithful and honest.

But if there is no reception or aspect and the planets are in unfortunate signs, the contrary may be expected.

Also, if the ruler of the fifth is combust or retrograde, then doubt his integrity or ability to perform the business.

Sixth House Questions

Of Servants, Lodgers, or Tenants in General

Take the first house, its ruler, and the Moon to signify the person who asked the question. The sixth house and its ruler to denote the person inquired about.

If the querent wishes to inquire about their honesty, etc., see if the ruler of the sixth is in good aspect to the ruler of the first or the Moon, or to a planet in the first house.

If the ruler of the sixth house cusp or a planet in the sixth house is making no aspect to the ruler of the first or planet in the first house, but the Moon translates the light of the ruler of the sixth to the first by any good aspect—this shows they will prove honest and trustworthy.

Do not trust them if the Sun is in the sixth house afflicted in Libra or Aquarius, or the ruler of the sixth is in the second and afflicted; the Moon ruler of the sixth house or in the sixth or square to the ruler of the sixth in the second, the person asked about will be mean in conduct, and will prove dishonest.

If the South Node is in the sixth or the ruler of the sixth in bad aspect to Uranus; the Moon in the Via combust degree and sign the same.

If the Moon translates the light from the ruler of the sixth to the first by bad aspect, do not engage the servant, rent to the person, or have any dealings with them.

If Mercury, the natural sixth house ruler, is retrograde, combust the Sun, conjunct the Moon, or in bad aspect to Uranus, Saturn or Mars, the person will either be dull or mentally unbalanced with bad disposition.

If the Moon is in Pisces afflicted, they prove unfaithful. If in Capricorn they are not to be depended upon.

If the Question Is About a Tenant's Removal

The first and its ruler is the querent; the sixth house and its ruler is the tenant.

Number the sixth house the first of the question; the seventh and its ruler denotes the substance or money of the tenant.

The ruler of the twelfth and its position in a sign shows whether the tenant will go; this twelfth is the seventh from the sixth or where they go.

If the cusps of the sixth and twelfth are movable, their rulers in movable signs or near the end of a sign, it shows the tenant will move.

They will move when the ruler of the sixth or twelfth or a planet in the twelfth leaves a sign or turns retrograde.

If the rulers of the twelfth, sixth, or tenth are in bad aspect to each other, the rent will be too high.

If the ruler of the seventh is afflicted by a planet in the seventh or to the ruler of the first, the same is true.

The ruler of the sixth afflicted by the ruler of the eighth, the neighbors make trouble for the tenant, as the eighth is the third from the sixth or the tenant's neighbors.

The natural twelfth house ruler, Neptune, if in the sixth, and afflicted in any way, shows treachery or trouble through all sixth house affairs.

How to Attain Health and What Causes Sickness

The signs of the zodiac and houses that Saturn and the Sun occupy in the horoscope of a man, and the Moon and Mars in a woman's, will show, when afflicted to malefics, the part of the body where disease or sickness is most likely to manifest.

First to be considered is what planet causes the disease; second, what part of the body is afflicted by the disease.

The zodiacal signs control the physiological functions. The planets control the anatomy or structure of the organisms of the human body.

In considering the pathology of disease or sickness, it is necessary to understand that each sign, when afflicted, naturally tends to excess that will eventually endanger the whole system.

The Sun gives us our constitution; it rules the heart, vitality, and arteries.

Destructive to the virtues of the Sun are Saturn and Mars, because wherever Saturn is, there will be poor circulation; so Saturn will lower the vitality.

Mars increases the vitality to fever-heat and therefore excites the nervous system.

The Moon rules the natural functions of the body; it rules the stomach, fluidic and lymphatic systems.

If the Sun and Moon are elevated above the malefics, there is less danger of disease and very little illness as we go through life.

The common signs affect the nervous system.

The cardinal signs affect the functional parts of the body.

The fixed signs point to organic weakness of the system.

The common signs and their rulers are to a great extent the pathology of all disease and sickness.

These signs and their rulers then would show the cure of all disease and sickness, because the common signs are the only signs that have their rulers, Mercury and Jupiter, in the natural zodiac always square and opposition to each other.

Another reason is that these signs fall in cadent houses in the natural zodiac.

Jupiter, ruler of Sagittarius and Pisces, rules, among other things, the liver. Jupiter nourishes the body and does so through the veins. The arterial blood is also governed by Jupiter; (Jupiter is exalted in Cancer).

Mercury is ruler of Gemini and Virgo and is exalted in Virgo (sixth house sign); Virgo rules, among other things, the intestinal tract.

Both Jupiter and Mercury rule the brain manifestations. Jupiter is said to rule the higher mind, Mercury the lower mind. Jupiter rules our judgment, which is supposed to reside in the middle of the brain and should rule over the other faculties to a great extent. Jupiter is the seat of reason and the guide of action.

Mercury is supposed to regulate or preserve harmony among all our senses. Mercury has rule over the vagus nerve (Mercury is exalted in Virgo).

Mercury then, to a big extent, rules our feelings and imagination because Mercury ramifies all over the body, is of all qualities, works directly with the Sun and Moon, and rules the signs Gemini and Virgo.

Gemini rises before the sign Cancer, and Virgo follows the sign

Leo. It is Mercury's nature to apply itself to any object; Mercury is considered a mutable planet.

If the judgment, Jupiter, is asleep, and the imagination, Mercury, runs at random, then thought, Saturn, cannot function intellectually.

Let us apply this analogy to the physical body and health. Jupiter rules over our appetites; the taste is at the root of the tongue on purpose, that we may extract all the nourishment from our food for the liver to convert into blood.

We should retain a normal mouthful of food long enough to extract all the nourishment from the food to be converted into energized blood; Mars is the energizer and Jupiter rules greed.

Connected with the great vagus nerve is found the pharyngeal plexus, which is the brains of, or controller of, the motive action of the constrictor or swallow muscles.

Here lies the seat of the greatest battle each person has to fight and conquer. The subduing of the mighty Tocea giant or Impulse which causes the facial gateway muscles to grab the food morsels before they are triturated enough in the mouth with the secretions which flow from the ducts of each cheek.

This takes place automatically in early childhood.

That is one of the reasons why the tongue is the magic reflector of the physiological status of the glands, the organs, etc.

The different colors of the tongue—shiny yellow, brown, white greyish, light brown, golden yellow, green brown—denote what is interfering with the natural organic action or clogging of the system.

Students should be familiar with what the common signs rule in the physiology of the body, that they may see why these signs, and planets ruling them, govern the cause of disease.

Neptune and Jupiter, ruler and co-ruler of Pisces, are exalted in

Cancer for a very special reason.

On all three planes—physical, mental and spiritual—Mercury is the planet that symbolizes body, soul, and spirit. We must perfect (Pisces) the body.

Neptune, the spiritual ruler of Pisces (if we think of Neptune as exalted in Leo, sign of the heart, ruled by the Sun), should open our eyes to spiritual truths.

Afflicted planets are simply misdirected energy. Ignorance impels us to do many things that wisdom transcends.

The living intelligent spirit, acting through the sympathetic nerves upon the muscular or tubular system, tries to throw off accumulating poisons and in doing so produces acute diseases which should be a healing crisis.

By using Mercury, the mental planet, and Jupiter, the higher mind, the spirit can be aroused to positive activity in eliminating poisons.

If we could understand and use intelligently the planets' exaltations, we could demonstrate spiritual mastery and keep the flesh subservient to the spirit.

All false habits of living, hereditary and other factors store the cells with useless substance that will and do cause disease and sickness unless we try to understand and live the Law.

How to Judge Questions Pertaining to Sickness and Disease in General

Questions of such nature follow the same procedure as all other questions. The ruler of the first, and in questions of such nature take the planet ruling the decanate of the rising sign; planets in the rising sign; a planet in the sixth or ruling the sixth house cusp; and the seventh house are to be considered for the person who asks the question.

If the ruler of the first, sixth or the Moon is in the fixed signs and in cadent houses, it shows the disease or sickness to be long and tedious. The rulers of these signs afflicting each other denote the same.

Common signs rising or on the cusps of succedent houses do not show long sickness unless the Moon is slow in motion and the ruler of the sixth is retrograde. If you do find the above, it will show the disease or sickness to be chronic.

If the ruler of the sixth is a malefic and badly afflicted in the sixth, eighth or twelfth, and, at the same time the hyleg is badly afflicted, there is not much hope of recovery.

If the ruler of the sixth is retrograde, in its fall or detriment, conjunct the Sun, or in the eighth conjunct, square, semi-square or opposition Saturn, Mars or Uranus, the sick person will probably never recover.

The Sun and Moon both cadent and their dispositors with the ruler of the first and afflicted shows either a dangerous or long tedious disease, depending on the signs they are in.

The ruler of the first in the sixth and the ruler of the sixth in the first denotes much sickness if these planets are afflicted. Always consider what planet or planets afflict either the Ascendant, its ruler, or the ruler of the sixth, and the planet the Moon afflicts.

Always consider the rulers of the sixth and twelfth and the planet from which the Moon last separated to denote what disease or sickness is manifesting at the time of the horary question.

If the Moon separates from the body of the malefics, Mars, Saturn, Uranus or Neptune in fixed signs, it would show accidents or some sudden calamity, especially if Mars is the ruler of the twelfth or sixth.

If the Moon separates from the body of Uranus or Mars or Saturn in common signs, and Venus is in the sixth or first and badly aspected, it shows the cause to be from over-indulgence, over-eating, the wrong kind of food, or a nervous breakdown.

If the Moon separates from the body of Mars and applies to Mercury, Saturn or Uranus in cardinal signs and Jupiter is ruler of the twelfth, the person is overworked and undernourished.

If the Moon or Mars is in a cardinal sign, square Saturn, Uranus or Neptune, the person will be in danger of a surgical operation.

There is always a dangerous time in any person's life for healing, and this time is when the eclipses afflict that person's Sun and Moon or planets by falling in the same degree of a sign as the natal planets are at birth.

The greatest danger is not at the time of the eclipse, but when Mars, Saturn, Uranus or Neptune transits by conjunction, square or opposition to this degree of the sign these planets are in at birth or by progression.

This will be within six months if it is a lunar eclipse or within twelve months if it is a solar eclipse.

Mars is the planet of greatest danger (of the so-called malefics) because it moves quickly through the signs. Ptolemy warns us not to have operations on that part of the body that corresponds to the sign that the Moon is in at birth or by progression or transit. He says: "Pierce not with iron that part of the body which may be governed by the sign actually occupied by the Moon."

Hyleg, Life and Death, and Medication

The length of our physical life is dependent on the position of the Sun, Moon and the rising sign and the planet ruling the Ascendant.

If they are in what is known as the hylegical places (called the hyleg) and afflicted by the malefics—Mars, Saturn, Uranus and Neptune—the life will be endangered, especially if the Sun by day and the Moon by night are in these places: the ninth, tenth, eleventh or seventh houses.

But if the Sun or Moon are not in these houses and are not afflicted as mentioned, then the Ascendant, its ruler or the Part of Fortune is counted as the hyleg.

But when the Sun and Moon and Ascendant are fortified by the benefics, a long life may be expected.

The Moon's Nodes—the Dragon's Head and the Dragon's Tail—have a great influence over the life and health. If the Dragon's Head is in the oriental part of the chart and conjunct Jupiter or Venus, it makes these planets stronger in their benefic influence; or if it is in the same degree as the Sun or the Moon and rising between the first and tenth, this strengthens the body.

But if with the malefics—Saturn, Mars, Uranus or Neptune—it gives a stronger indication to prove unfortunate for the health.

The Dragon's Tail hinders the benefic planets, and if in the same position in the chart, shows the opposite effect. These Nodes retrograde through the signs and complete their revolution every eighteen years.

A long life is indicated if the ruler of the first is stronger by sign and better aspected than the rulers of the sixth, eighth or twelfth; also, if Jupiter is parallel, conjunct, sextile or trine the ruler of the sixth and the Sun is not afflicted by the malefics.

If Venus, Jupiter, the Sun or Moon is in the first and not afflicted to or by the ruler of the eighth, the person never fears death.

The Moon in the tenth, well aspected to Saturn, Mars or Uranus denotes long life, but the Moon here shows that the person will have vomiting spells.

If the Moon separates from the ruler of the eighth and applies immediately to the Sun in the first, seventh, tenth or eleventh, it shows sudden recovery for the sick.

Death may be indicated if the ruler of the first and the Moon are conjunct the ruler of the eighth in the first, tenth, seventh or fourth, if the ruler of the eighth is a malefic.

If the ruler of the first separates from a conjunction of the ruler of the eighth by retrograde motion, when they come conjunct by direct motion, the sick person may not recover, unless the Sun is well aspected to the Ascendant or by these planets.

The Moon or Sun in the fourth, conjunct the malefics, indicates death; the Moon on the cusp of the first, square or opposition to Mars from the fourth, indicates the same.

The Moon conjunction the Sun in the eighth or conjunction the ruler of the sixth in the eighth, and the ruler of the eighth afflicted could indicate death. If the ruler of the first is with a malefic and another malefic planet is in the first, it could denote death in some form.

The ruler of the first under Earth and at the same time in bad aspect to the ruler of the eighth; if these two rulers are conjunct in the fourth; if the ruler of the first and eighth are the same planet, cadent and afflicted by the malefics, this denotes a dangerous condition.

It is considered best to give medicine when the Moon is in Cancer, Scorpio or Pisces, and if any of the above signs is under the Earth, the medicine given at such time is supposed to be beneficial.

If a person is sick and asks a question concerning a doctor, the rising sign and its ruler denotes the sick person.

The sign on the seventh house and its ruler denote the doctor or physician.

If the Moon or ruler of the seventh afflict the ruler of the first, the doctor or physician will not cure the patient.

The ruler of the tenth denotes the remedy or method the doctor employs for a cure.

If the ruler of the tenth afflicts the first in the same way, this shows that the medicine or whatever remedy the doctor employs is injurious to the patient.

If the ruler of the seventh is well aspected to the ruler of the first and at the same time the ruler of the tenth in any bad aspect, this shows that the doctor could eventually help the sick person by changing his prescription.

In the natal chart the sign on the cusp of the ninth house and its ruler usually shows what kind of treatment the individual requires for his specific benefit.

The Physical Health

The sixth house is the pathology of disease or sickness. The sign occupying the sixth house cusp is a general indication of the ailment caused by each sign.

Aries indicates the ailment will arise from the condition of the brain and causes headaches, neuralgia, insomnia and brain trouble. Trouble with the eyes and face is also indicated.

Taurus causes disorders through the condition of the throat—tonsillitis, diphtheria. The heart, bladder and excretory system are also influenced by reflex action.

Gemini causes trouble through the lungs, bronchial tubes, the respiratory and nervous system generally. It shows the lungs are the weakest part and the blood should be kept in good order and in good circulation.

Cancer disease arises through the condition of the stomach and digestive organs, causing fermentation of food stuff, gastric troubles, etc.

Leo causes trouble through inharmonious living, excesses that will disturb the heart and blood; this in turn acts on the throat and excretory system.

Virgo shows that the condition of the bowels is chief cause of the trouble; colic, constipation, dysentery and indigestion are likely to manifest.

Libra brings trouble through the condition of the kidneys and such disorders as diabetes; Bright's Disease and suppression of the urine are indicated.

Scorpio denotes that the condition of the excretory system, generative organs and bladder will be the chief cause of sickness; piles; secret disorders; retention of urine and inflammatory diseases are peculiar to this sign.

Sagittarius shows the condition of the blood and nervous system will have much to do with the health and ailments such as consumption, blood troubles, and disorders of the liver will manifest.

Capricorn shows colds, chills, poor circulation, and all tendencies to melancholia to be the cause of health troubles, which will be chiefly rheumatism, gout, constipation and skin diseases.

Aquarius denotes that the blood circulation and mental faculties will be the cause of sickness; eye trouble and all spasmodic and nervous complaints are indicated by Aquarius.

Pisces causes trouble to arise through carelessness in personal cleanliness, impurities of the blood and bad magnetism; all complaints of a tumorous nature come from this influence—also consumption and ailments of the fluidic system.

The Moon is the hyleg, or giver of life, in all female charts of health. According to the Moon's position and aspects, so will the general health and prospects of long life be.

The general health will be stronger when the Moon is above the horizon than when below the horizon. The two best signs for the Moon to occupy are Cancer and Pisces. The airy signs are good for the Moon, while Taurus and Virgo, of the earth signs, give strength to the constitution and general health.

The fiery signs are not so favorable for the Moon as these signs do not harmonize with the Moon's nature. The two worst signs for the Moon are Scorpio and Capricorn.

Scorpio produces impurities, irregularities of the female organs, and is indicative of bad habits that will eventually react on the health. Capricorn weakens the Moon's power, and those born while the Moon is in this sign are generally weak and delicate, especially when young.

When the Moon afflicts the Sun it causes general debility of the health, irregularities of the system through colds and chills. This is considered a bad affliction for females.

The Moon afflicting Mercury causes mental troubles caused by worry, etc.

The Moon afflicting Venus indicates irregularities and troubles arising through carelessness, excesses and indiscretions.

The Moon afflicting Mars denotes fevers, accidents, inflammatory disorders, painful irregularities, and complaints due to rashness. This is a particularly evil influence for females.

The Moon afflicting Jupiter causes blood and liver trouble, irregularities caused by over-indulgence and high living, wrong eating.

The Moon afflicting Saturn denotes long, lingering and chronic complaints caused from colds, chills, neglect and debility of the body.

The Moon afflicting Uranus causes nervous strain and accidents.

The Moon afflicting Neptune causes disorders of a mental nature and ailments affecting the fluidic system.

Psychic disorders are also caused by Neptune's afflictions.

The Sun is hyleg, or giver of life, in all male horoscopes of health. According to the Sun's position and aspects so will the general health and prospects of long life be.

When the Sun is above the horizon the general health will be stronger than if the Sun should be below the horizon.

The Sun is stronger when placed in positive signs and weaker in negative signs. Libra and Aquarius are the weakest of the positive signs, while Taurus and Scorpio are strongest of the negative signs.

The Sun in fiery signs is the strongest for health and long life; the vitality is much stronger than in any other sign. Illness will be sharp and severe but soon over.

The airy signs are the next strongest, but the health is weakened by worry and nervous complaints. The health will soon improve through mental rest and changes of scenery.

The earth signs give a solid constitution but illness is likely to be long and severe and recovery usually slow. Capricorn is not so strong in early childhood.

The Sun in water signs gives the weakest constitutions with the exception of Scorpio. These signs are too receptive to outside influences; Scorpio has too much magnetic power.

The Sun's affliction to Venus is only a semi-square aspect and therefore not very strong but does show the tendencies to indiscretion and excess.

The Sun afflicting Mars increases the vitality but causes fevers, inflammatory disorders, cuts, wounds and accidents.

The Sun afflicting Jupiter causes blood disorders, apoplexy and all complaints due to high living and excesses in the diet.

The Sun afflicting Saturn causes chronic disorders, lingering complaints, illnesses arising from cold neglect and privation. This is the worst affliction the Sun can have.

The Sun afflicting Uranus causes incurable diseases, accidents, peculiar nervous and brain affections.

The Sun afflicting Neptune causes psychic disorders, wasting of tissue and drug-taking.

The disorders of the planet Mercury when placed in the sixth house in the twelve signs is as follows:

In Aries: headaches; facial neuralgia; insomnia and all nervous affections of the head.

In Taurus: Throat troubles; nerve affections; hoarseness; vocal disorders; convulsions during dentition.

In Gemini: Defects of the respiratory system; bronchitis; nerve pains in the shoulders, arms and hands; cramps in the feet.

In Cancer: Spasms, colic, flatulency and digestive troubles due to worry and anxiety.

In Leo: Pains in the spinal nerves; palpitation of the heart due to bad blood.

In Virgo: Diarrhoea, obstruction and colic in bowels; worms and intestinal irritation.

In Libra: Neuralgia of the kidneys; urinary obstructions.

In Scorpio: Disorders of the nerves in the privy parts; neuralgia and disorders of the generative organs.

In Sagittarius: Sciatica; nervousness and weakness of hips and thighs.

In Capricorn: Constipation and bowel troubles due to worry and melancholic tendencies; rheumatism; gout.

In Aquarius: Hysteria and general debility of the nervous system.

In Pisces: Poor circulation; cold feet; consumption; corns, bunions, callouses.

Venus in the sixth house will in general protect the health unless badly afflicted to the Ascendant or planet ruling the rising sign.

In Aries: eczema; skin troubles; bad complexion; irritation due to cosmetics.

In Taurus: Throat troubles; mumps; goitre; abscesses; quinsy.

In Gemini: Irregular respiration due to the wrong kind of

clothes.

In Cancer: Indigestion; surfeit; sick stomach; dizzy spells.

In Leo: Heart trouble; swoons; palpitation due to tight clothes.

In Virgo: Worms; lactic acid; irregularities of the bowels; intestinal trouble due to wrong diet and bad habits in eating.

In Libra: Diabetes; eczema; kidney trouble.

In Scorpio: Womb disorders; venereal troubles; weakness of the bladder; disease of the ovaries and of the vaginal passage.

In Sagittarius: Lung trouble; gout in the hips.

In Capricorn: Constipation; skin disorders; knee trouble.

In Aquarius: Hysteria; anaemia; poorness of the blood. Venus in Aquarius weakens the red blood corpuscles causing dropsy.

In Pisces: If much afflicted, disorders through intemperance; tumors; tender feet; bunions.

The chief disorders of Mars in the sixth house in each of the twelve signs follows:

In Aries: Brain fever; ruptured blood vessels in the brain; cerebral congestion; ringworm; smallpox; inflammation of the eyes.

In Taurus: Stone in the bladder; diphtheria; tonsillitis; inflammation of the larynx; erysipelas.

In Gemini: Inflammation of the lungs; bronchitis; pneumonia; impurities of the blood; boils on the neck and arms.

In Cancer: Bilious complaints; gastric fevers; typhoid; hemorrhage of the stomach. With females, Mars here gives great danger in child birth and abortions.

In Leo: Pleurisy; malarial fever; palpitation of the heart.

In Virgo: Cholera; diarrhoea; dysentery; inflammation of the bowels; peritonitis; appendicitis; hernia.

In Libra: Pains in the lumbar region, inflammation of the kidneys and a tendency to fevers due to disordered kidneys.

In Scorpio: Fistulas; piles; venereal diseases; stone in bladder; gout; septic poisoning in females; inflammation of womb; hemorrhage; abortions.

In Sagittarius: Ulcers of hips or thighs; sciatica; inflammation of lungs; boils, and trouble with the anus.

In Capricorn: Yellow jaundice; dysentery; skin diseases; rheumatism; inflammation of the knee joints.

In Aquarius: Erysipelas; blood poisoning; varicose veins in the legs; ulcers of the legs; palpitation of the heart.

In Pisces: Tumorous complaints; consumption; infections and complaints due to intemperance, family interference.

Jupiter in the sixth house in each of the twelve signs follows:

In Aries: Congestion of the brain; dizziness; swoons.

In Taurus: Distemper in the throat; complaints caused by gluttony and over-indulgence in eating; gout.

In Gemini: Lung afflictions; pleurisy; blood disorders.

In Cancer: Indigestion; flatulency; scurvy dropsy.

In Leo: Feverish and over-heated state of the blood; pleurisy; faulty degeneration of the heart; palpitation.

In Virgo: Liver troubles; impurities of the blood; weakness of the bowels; abscesses on the liver or bowels; jaundice.

In Libra: Diabetes; tumors in the reins; kidney troubles; obstructions.

In Scorpio: Abscesses; dropsy; piles; urinary and seminal complaints.

In Sagittarius: Sciatica; pains and swelling in the legs and hips; gout.

In Capricorn: Sluggish circulation of the blood; eczema and skin trouble.

In Aquarius: Blood poisoning; lumbago; over-abundance of blood in system.

In Pisces: Tumorous disorders; dropsical complaints; poor condition of the blood.

Saturn in the sixth house in each of the twelve signs follows:

In Aries: Toothache; colds in the head; cerebral troubles; deafness; head, stomach and liver troubles.

In Taurus: Laryngitis and disorders of the gullet; diphtheria; quinsy; mumps; loss of voice.

In Gemini: Disorders of the respiratory system; rheumatic afflictions of the arms and shoulders; consumption; pneumonia.

In Cancer: Cancer in the breast; stomach ulcers; gastric, digestive and asthmatic complaints; and in females, affection of the womb.

In Leo: Spinal trouble; gout; liver complaints; organic weakness of the heart; jaundice.

In Virgo: Constipation; obstruction in the bowels; malnutrition; catarrh of the bowels and colic.

In Libra: Blood disorders; renal affections; suppression of the urine; lumbago; Bright's Disease; head and kidney trouble.

In Scorpio: Piles; fistula; gravel; stone; gout; retention of urine.

In Sagittarius: Consumption; bronchitis; gout; sciatica; hip-joint diseases; debility of the nervous system.

In Capricorn: Skin diseases; constipation and bowel complaints; rheumatism; ague; all painful and chronic troubles affecting the knee joints.

In Aquarius: Spinal trouble; weak circulation of the blood; affections of the eyes, ankles and legs; cramps; anaemia.

In Pisces: Danger of taking cold through getting wet feet; consumption; catarrh; gout; bunions; rheumatism.

Uranus in the sixth house in each of the twelve signs follows:

In Aries: Paralysis of the facial nerves; spasmodic pains in the head; inflammation of the coverings and membranes of the brain.

In Taurus: Trouble with the vocal cords and motor nerves of the throat.

In Gemini: Asthma; cramp in the arms and shoulders.

In Cancer: Cancer in the stomach; mental illusion; cramp of the stomach.

In Leo: Stoppage of heart's action or sudden death; cramp of the heart.

In Virgo: Spasm; cramps in the bowels.

In Libra: Disorders of the kidneys, spasmodic lumbago.

In Scorpio: Cancer of the generative system; deformities of the womb in females; spasm of the bladder.

In Sagittarius: Cramp in the hips and thighs; sciatica.

In Capricorn. Deformities of the knees; cramps in the knees.

In Aquarius: Nervous disorders; hysteria; cramps in the ankles; varicose veins.

In Pisces: Feet sweating; bunions; trouble with metatarsals.

Neptune in the sixth house in each of the twelve signs follows:

In Aries: Brain trouble and delusions; drug habits.

In Taurus: Septic poison in the throat; affections of the eyes.

In Gemini: Consumption and wasting of the system.

In Cancer: Dipsomania; hypochondria.

In Leo: Suspension of the heart action.

In Virgo: Malnutrition; consumption of the bowels; appendicitis.

In Libra: Dropsy.

In Scorpio: Venereal diseases.

In Sagittarius: Nervous disorders; consumption.

In Capricorn: Leprosy; skin diseases.

In Aquarius: Obsession; nervous affections.

In Pisces: Dropsy; disorders of the fluidic system.

Questions Concerning Small Animals Such as Chickens, Turkeys, Sheep, Pigs, Calves, Birds, Dogs, Cats, and Pets

Success with small animals is indicated if the ruler of the first and sixth are parallel, conjunct, sextile or trine each other, and if the ruler of the sixth makes any good aspect to the Part of Fortune; or if the Moon is conjunct the Part of Fortune in the sixth house.

Mercury, natural ruler of the sixth house, should be well dignified, and the Moon should be in good aspect to Mercury for success in such questions.

No luck or gain is shown if the South Node is in the sixth or if a retrograde, combust or peregrine planet is there.

Saturn retrograde in the sixth house shows that they will die of a disease or epidemic.

Mars there shows accidents with animals and losses through theft, bad bargains or the owner's carelessness.

Questions Concerning Lost, Strayed or Stolen Animals

The animal will be found or returned if the ruler of the sixth is making a good aspect to the ruler of the first, if the Moon is in good aspect or translating the light from the ruler of the first to the ruler of the sixth. A planet well-dignified in the sixth; if the ruler of the sixth is well dignified in the second, fifth or eleventh house in good aspect to Jupiter, Venus or the Sun; or if the ruler of the sixth is in the first. In a question of this kind the ruler of the sixth retrograde shows a return of the animal.

The rules given for lost articles apply also to lost animals; the directions and places one should look are shown by the signs and houses.

When considering the purchase of animals or pets, a favorable time is indicated if the Moon is in Taurus, Cancer, Virgo, or Pisces, and if the Moon is separating from a malefic and applying to a parallel or good aspect to Venus, Jupiter, the Part of Fortune, or the ruler of the Ascendant.

Venus in the sixth house usually indicates that the person loves animals, especially cats and birds.

A person with Jupiter and Saturn in good aspect is able to train or tame almost any animal.

It is my personal opinion that we can learn much from animals; it is a well known fact that a person who loves animals and is kind to them has many fine qualities. Animals instinctively sense this quality and are antagonistic or friendly, accordingly.

Seventh House Questions

Questions About Love and Marriage

The Moon, Venus and Mars in aspect in a man's chart or the Sun, Mars and Venus in a woman's chart will bring love and marriage. This is always by application, for when the planets are separating, it shows what is past; by application, that which is to come.

A man and woman will marry, it makes no difference which one asks the question, and the rules are the same provided the chart is radical.

If the Sun and Moon are in good aspect to Jupiter, Venus, Mars, or the ruler of the seventh house; the ruler of the seventh or first in the seventh, fifth, tenth or eleventh and in good aspect with the ruler of the Ascendant; the ruler of the first, Venus, Mars or Moon in the seventh, also if the ruler of the seventh is in the first; if the rulers of the seventh or the Sun or Mars is in Cancer, Scorpio, or Pisces; if the rulers of the first and seventh are in good aspect to each other, then the couple will marry.

If the ruler of the first is in the seventh in its fall or detriment, shows the party to be very anxious to marry.

If Uranus, Saturn or Mars is ruler of the seventh and in the first, shows the person to be uneasy about or unsure of the sweetheart or lover.

If the ruler of the seventh and the ruler of the first are in their fall or detriment, it shows that the person is careless about the matter or desperate about the circumstances concerned in their relationship.

Will the Woman Marry?

The woman will not marry if the Sun has left or is applying to a bad aspect of Uranus or Saturn; this shows that she probably will repel rather than attract the opposite sex. If the Sun is in aspect to Mars by trine or sextile, or Mars is trine or sextile Uranus, she will fascinate him, especially if the Sun or Mars is in a fiery or watery sign.

If the ruler of the first or the Sun or Mars is in Gemini, Leo, or Virgo, and especially if they are square or opposition each other, or to the ruler of the seventh, or if Mars is afflicted or weak, it will be long before she marries.

The ruler of the first, Sun or Mars in its fall or detriment, she either cares nothing about it or despairs of being married.

If the ruler of the first is conjunct the Sun, or the ruler of the first or the ruler of the seventh is conjunct the Sun in the first, tenth or eleventh; ruler of the first in the seventh and fortunate; the ruler of the first and the Sun sextile or trine from the eleventh, seventh or fifth or ninth, she will marry.

Planets and Aspects that Hinder Marriage

If the planets signifying marriage are applying to a good aspect to each other and a malefic planet collects the aspect from either of these rulers before they complete their good aspect, the marriage will be hindered.

Observe the house of which this interfering planet is the ruler and where it is placed. If it is ruler of the second, the hindrance will be about money or second house affairs.

If it is the ruler of the third, it will show the cause to be relatives or neighbors or short journeys or gossip, etc.

The fourth house ruler shows the father or mother to be the cause; or it may be about a house question or settlement of land, etc.

The fifth shows children would cause trouble; that either of the parties would cheat or whatever the fifth house denotes.

The sixth would indicate sickness or opposition from some relative—aunt or uncle—or private enemy of the seventh house person (as the sixth is the twelfth from the seventh). It might show trouble through a child by another marriage.

The seventh or planet in the seventh denotes a public enemy, a lawsuit or a rival.

The ruler of the eighth denotes lack of money, and, if another aspect occurs at the same time, it may be caused by death and thus prevent marriage. The ninth shows hindrance and trouble through blood relatives of the seventh house party. It could be interference of some lawyer, religious differences, or the first house person might go on a long journey or voyage and hinder the marriage.

The tenth shows interference by some person having authority over the parties involved.

The eleventh shows the friends of both the parties dislike the match, or that a previous marriage may have been contracted by either party and in some way cause trouble. The twelfth or a planet there shows underhandedness, double-dealing, or secret scandal that causes enmity between them.

Chances are the parties to be married will never know just what separated them or just where or who started the scandal that caused them to separate. Now in this manner the student can ascertain who will assist or hinder the parties wishing to marry.

The Time the Marriage Will Take Place

This is shown by the degrees between the ruler of the first and the ruler of the seventh by parallel, conjunction, sextile or trine, or, of the ruler of the seventh from the cusp of the first by conjunction or parallel; the degree between the ruler of the seventh or the Moon to Venus or the Sun, or the Sun to a parallel or good aspect to Mars; a square or opposition of the ruler of the first and seventh if they are in mutual reception and especially in angles.

The time must be judged according to the degree of distance the rulers are from each other by application according to the "measure of time."

Here is something to prove in charts. If a woman is born between sunrise and noon (if her Sun is rising between the first and tenth house), or between sunset and midnight (if her Sun is between the seventh and fourth house) she will usually marry early in life, or marry a man younger than herself.

If she is born between noon and sunset, or between midnight and sunrise, she generally marries late in life, or to a person many years her senior. Of course, aspects will modify or accentuate this rule.

In the chart of a male, take the Moon and judge the same way you judged the Sun for the woman.

The student will find these rules in various astrological textbooks. I have used them for years with success; you may do likewise. None of us can take credit for the foundation or the principles of astrology, as they belong to Universal Mind. We interpret them according to our understanding and experience.

How the Parties Will Agree in Marriage

They will agree if the ruler of the first or the Moon is conjunct, parallel, sextile or trine the ruler of the seventh or Venus; the Moon in conjunction with Jupiter or Venus, they are industrious. Jupiter or Venus well placed in the seventh, or even the ruler of the seventh, square the ruler of the first (but they must be in mutual reception) indicates agreement. The Moon in good aspect to her disposer by house or exaltation shows the same.

The rulers of the first and seventh in square or opposition, or the Moon afflicted, in bad aspect to the ruler of the first, Uranus, Saturn, Mars or the South Node in the seventh; or these malefics in the first, the querent is to blame for the trouble in marriage or is unconventional, according to the sign ascending.

The Moon in its fall, square or opposition of the malefics, or any retrograde planet, the man is to blame. The Sun in its fall, square or opposition of the malefics, the woman is to blame.

The ruler of the seventh angular and a heavier planet than the ruler of the first, the partner strives for mastery.

Venus afflicted by Uranus, Saturn, Mars or the South Node or

Venus retrograde or in its fall, the man suffers most. The Moon afflicted, they both suffer. Uranus, Saturn, Mars or the South Node afflicted in the tenth or fourth shows continual quarrels, or separation caused by the parents.

Any planet afflicting the ruler of the first or seventh in the third shows trouble through neighbors or relations; in the fourth or tenth, the parents; in the fifth, loose morals or children; in the sixth, a servant, person visiting, or a roomer; in the seventh, open enemies; in the second or eighth, money difficulties; in the ninth, the in-laws or religious differences.

Venus and Saturn in conjunction, aspecting Mars, shows jealousy. The Moon void of course and in conjunction of the ruler of the eighth or in the twelfth with Uranus, Saturn, Mars or the South Node, one of them may die or have some misfortune.

Which of the Two Is Best Connected

See whether the ruler of the first, the querent's significator, or the ruler of the seventh is better placed and so judge.

The querent is the best connected if the ruler of the first is in the tenth, first, seventh or fourth, and the ruler of the seventh is in the second, fifth, eleventh or eighth.

But a more certain way to judge is by observing which of the two significators is the most powerful or better dignified.

Will the Querent Marry More Than Once?

If the querent's significators are in double-bodied signs, he will marry more than once; and the same if they are joined with or apply to many planets, particularly from the fifth, seventh or eleventh houses.

Many planets in the seventh, or in good aspect with the ruler of the first, or the Sun or Moon, are all signs of repeated marriage.

If the significators are in fixed signs or in aspect to only one planet, the querent will marry but once. In this case, take the Moon for the man and the Sun for the woman, to the ruler of the first.

If the Sun and Moon have no application, or but one, the querent will never marry, or but once, even if the ruler of the first is ever so well aspected.

Whether Man or Wife Will Die First

The ruler of the first and the Moon denote the querent, and the ruler of the eighth his death, etc. The ruler of the seventh denotes the partner and the ruler of the second his or her death.

See which significators, that is, the rulers of the first and eighth, or seventh and second, are first in conjunction with the Sun, that person will probably die first; in Aries, Cancer, Libra or Capricorn shows death shortly; in Gemini, Virgo, Sagittarius or Pisces, longer before death; Leo, Scorpio, Taurus or Aquarius, many years before death.

The one whose significator is angular or strong in dignities, free from affliction or combustion, or free from the ruler of the eighth, that party will live longest, especially if in good aspect with Jupiter or Venus; he or she will outlive the other by several years, except the parties are both very aged—then the survivor's health will be good.

The querent will die first if the ruler of the first or eighth first applies to the conjunction of the Sun; or if retrograde or in its fall; or if the ruler of the first is in the first, or Jupiter is in conjunction, square, or opposition to either ruler; or if the ruler of the sixth or twelfth is Uranus, Saturn or Mars.

The partner dies first if the ruler of the second or seventh is in the above condition; but if the ruler of the first or eighth is in the above condition, then the querent will die first.

Has the Lady Another Affair?

She is interested in another man if her ruler is in conjunction, sextile or trine any other planet than that which significates the querent; if several planets are in the seventh or the Sun aspects many planets or is conjunct Mars; if the Sun or ruler of the seventh is conjunct Mars or Jupiter and the North Node is in the seventh. The South Node in the seventh denotes trouble, or discreditable desire.

The ruler of the seventh with Saturn, she loves an elderly person; if with Uranus a mechanic, engineer or author; if with Jupiter a pretended religionist or a professional man; if with Mercury, a clerk, writer or bookseller.

But she has only one, if the ruler of the seventh is void of course or with the North Node or if no planet is in the seventh; the ruler of the seventh aspecting only the ruler of the first; Mars in the seventh, unless it is in its own sign or house.

The description of the person may be found by the planet signifying the party, considering at the same time the sign in which that planet is located.

Has the Gentleman Another Affair?

He is interested in another when any planet is in the seventh and not the ruler of the seventh. The ruler of the seventh or the Moon with Venus, she is very giddy; if sextile or trine, the lady loves him; but if the Moon or ruler of the seventh does not dispose of Venus, she does not care for him.

If either the ruler of the seventh or the Moon is conjunct the rising sign, and the Moon separates from the ruler of the first, he has another affair.

The ruler of the seventh separating from one to three degrees from any planet except the ruler of the first; the ruler of the seventh or the Moon conjunction the North Node or South Node, or any planet with them; the ruler of the seventh and Venus conjunction in Scorpio, or Taurus especially in the seventh, he has more than one affair.

If the Moon or ruler of the seventh is conjunct Mars, Jupiter or

Mercury, he has one described by that planet, and her age may be known by the number of degrees the planet is advanced in the sign. If with Mercury, she is a teacher of youth; if with Saturn, he loves an elderly person; if they separate, he is leaving her; if with the Sun, it is a person of consequence; if with Uranus, Venus or the Sun, he is changeable.

Will the Husband or Wife Return

The ruler of the seventh or ninth retrograde, either in the first or applying to the ruler of the first; the ruler of the first in the seventh unafflicted; a translation of light between the rulers of the first and seventh denotes a return.

The Moon increasing or in good aspect to the ruler of the first, especially if from the first; the Moon separating from Jupiter, Venus, or the North Node and applying to an aspect of Uranus, Saturn, Mars or the South Node; the ruler of the seventh combust; the ruler of the first aspecting the malefics, the person will be found against his will, or will be forced to return.

The ruler of the seventh with a stationary planet in an angle or succedent house, he or she is confused about what to do. The Moon separating from the ruler of the first and going to a conjunction of the ruler of the seventh, the person will be heard of.

The Moon aspecting her own house with a sextile or trine shows return or that the person will be heard of in two or three days. The ruler of the seventh or Mercury combust in the twelfth shows danger of imprisonment.

The ruler of the seventh applying to the Sun or to the ruler of the first shows a return.

A Woman Leaving Her Husband

The Sun under the Earth; Venus between the fourth and first and retrograde; also the ruler of the first, the Moon and the ruler of the seventh in trine shows she will return.

The ruler of the first, the Moon and the ruler of the seventh square or opposition without reception, she will not return. Mars in an angle, disposing of the Moon and, at the same time, the ruler of the first in Aries, Cancer, Libra or Capricorn, they are content to separate.

Reverse these rules and use the Moon and Venus for a man leaving a woman.

May I Enter Into Partnership or Society?

Note: Most of these questions will be similar to those on marriage.

The ruler of the first and the Moon denote the querent, and the second and its ruler his money matters.

The ruler of the seventh denotes the other person, and the ruler of the eighth shows his money.

The tenth house denotes the honor, credit, benefit, etc. from the partnership.

The fourth house and its ruler denotes the circumstances of this partnership, whether good or otherwise and how long it will last.

The partnership will do well if the rulers of the first and seventh are in good aspect or mutual reception; if the rulers of the first and seventh are not applying to each other, but in mutual reception; or if the Moon translates the light from one ruler to the other. If the rulers are in Taurus, Leo, Scorpio or Aquarius, more especially if there is mutual reception, you will agree, and the partnership or society will last. If in Aries, Cancer, Libra or Capricorn, without reception, you will have many contentions and disagreements; at other times you will agree, yet you will mistrust each other and no great gain can be expected. The ruler in Gemini, Virgo, Sagittarius or Pisces is a symbol of good.

The cause of disagreement can be determined as follows: See what house the afflicting planet is ruler of; if it is the ruler of the sixth, evil servants defraud or make strife between you; if rulers of the second or eighth, money matters are bad; and so judge according to the ruler of the house over which the afflicted planet rules.

An evil planet in the tenth or its ruler afflicted shows no trade or that you cannot dispose of the commodities.

Shall We Succeed in Business Partnership?

The ruler of the tenth strong, and a fortunate planet, well aspected, shows success. The Moon applying to a good aspect of the benefics or to the ruler of the tenth and not afflicted or retrograde; and good planets in the tenth denote prosperity.

The business will not be very successful if the South Node is in the tenth; if malefic planets aspect the ruler of the seventh and first; or if the ruler of the tenth is unfortunately situated or aspected.

Which Will Be the Best Qualified?

If the ruler of the first is more dignified than the ruler of the seventh, and better aspected, it denotes the querent will be the most benefitted by the partnership; but if the ruler of the seventh is more dignified, the quesited gains most.

Mars or Mercury ruler of the second or the South Node there, afflicting the ruler of the eighth, the querent will cheat; but if Mars or Mercury is ruler of the eighth, or the South Node is there, afflicting the ruler of the second, the quesited will cheat.

That planet which afflicts the Part of Fortune will waste the common stock. An evil planet in the first, the querent is false; but in the seventh, the quesited is not to be trusted, and he is in poor circumstances.

He whose significators are strongest will prosper and be the most fortunate; and he whose significators are weakest will be injured, if these rulers are posited in evil places in the figure.

If the Moon separates from a good planet and applies to an evil one, although a good beginning is made, it will nevertheless end in debate and strife.

If the Moon separates from an evil planet and applies to another, it signifies a bad beginning and a worse ending.

A benefic planet in the fourth or the ruler of the fourth in good aspect to the ruler of the first, second, seventh, eighth or the Part of Fortune, denotes a good end. Read the fourth house for the rest of the judgment.

Retrograde or peregrine planets are evil. If the ruler of the seventh or eighth is retrograde the querent's affairs are desperate, and he wishes to improve them; if in the sixth, peregrine, have nothing to do with him, unless there is application between the ruler of the seventh and Jupiter.

Lawsuits

The ruler of the first, the Sun and the Moon signify the querent.

The seventh house and its ruler signify the adversary.

The ruler of the tenth denotes the lawyer, etc.

The ruler of the fourth and the Moon's application show the result.

You May Prevent a Lawsuit and Be Reconciled

If the ruler of the first or the Moon is unafflicted and in good aspect with the ruler of the seventh, or in mutual reception, you will agree.

If the ruler of the seventh disposes of the ruler of the first; or the ruler of the first disposes of the ruler of the seventh you will agree by means of some person's help.

If the ruler of the first and seventh aspect the same planet, you will be reconciled by a third party.

Who Will Win the Lawsuit?

If the rulers of the first and seventh are afflicted by the malefic planets, neither party will win. The one whose ruler is more powerful or better aspected will be the victor. If the ruler of the first applies to the ruler of the seventh or if the ruler of the first is retrograde, the querent will be compelled to accept the verdict and agree to it.

If both the rulers are in angles and equally dignified, neither will submit and both will suffer.

If the ruler of the first is badly afflicted, retrograde, Via combust or in its detriment or fall, especially if the ruler of the seventh disposes of the ruler of the first, the adversary will win.

If the Moon applies to a benefic aspect of the ruler of the seventh or eighth and to malefic aspect of the ruler of the first or second, the adversary will overcome through scheming and evasion.

The querent will overcome if the ruler of the seventh is retrograde, via combust or afflicted in the first; if the Sun or Moon is in the first or aspects the ruler of the first; if the Moon applies to a parallel or good aspect of the ruler of the first and to a bad aspect of the ruler of the seventh; if the ruler of the fourth is in bad aspect to the ruler of the seventh or eighth.

How the Judge or Lawyer Will Decide the Case

If the ruler of the tenth is Uranus or Saturn, he will either not decide or the case will be moved to another court. If the ruler of the tenth is retrograde, he will not act fairly. If Uranus or Saturn rules the tenth, and Venus, the Sun, Mercury or the Moon are in any aspect except an opposition, the judge will probably set the case for another calendar date. If Mars opposes Uranus or Saturn, the judge will have a bad character, and if the Sun is in square of opposition to Uranus or Saturn, he may be disgraced.

If any planet is in the tenth and not the ruler of the tenth, undignified, and unaspected to the ruler of the tenth, the parties will not be satisfied. If Gemini, Virgo or Pisces is on the Ascendant or seventh house cusp, the case will be moved to another court.

If the ruler of the tenth makes a bad aspect to the ruler of the first, the judge will decide against the querent; to the seventh, he will rule against the adversary.

Aries, Cancer, Libra or Capricorn on the cusp of the seventh house, the parties may become reconciled by their own prudence.

The Moon translating the light from the ruler of the seventh to the ruler of the first shows that a third person will bring about a reconciliation. If the rulers of the first and seventh make no aspect to each other but both aspect a heavier planet, the parties will become reconciled by a third person described by that planet and the sign in which it is placed. Many times the judge is the means of reconciliation. Apply the rules given in the hindrance of marriage to see who hinders or reconciles the parties in lawsuits.

Will the Bankruptcy Action Be Successful?

The ruler of the first and the Moon signify the querent. The seventh, its ruler, and planets in the seventh denote the opponents or creditors. This question is judged much the same as lawsuits.

If the ruler of the first or the Moon is well placed and unafflicted, or the Moon and the ruler of the first in good aspect with the ruler of the tenth or fourth or with Venus or the Sun, then the querent succeeds.

But if the ruler of the seventh is unafflicted or in good aspect to the ruler of the fourth, tenth, or to Venus, Jupiter or the Sun, the creditors overcome. The person whose ruler is most afflicted will be the greatest loser.

If the ruler of the first is the strongest in every way and should at the same time be retrograde, it denotes the querent will be put back for a third or fourth hearing but will pass when that significator becomes direct, elevated or in good aspect with the ruler of the fourth or tenth house.

If Mercury is the ruler of the fourth or ninth, then the lawyer has not made the case sufficiently clear. This is especially so if Mercury is retrograde.

On the Recovery of Debts

The first, its ruler and the Moon signify the querent. The seventh and its ruler denote the debtor.

The eighth, which is the debtor's second, and its ruler, denote his means of paying.

If the ruler of the first is a benefic, the Moon conjunction or in good aspect with the ruler of the eighth or with a planet in the eighth; the ruler of the eighth a benefic and in the first or second, applying to a good aspect of the first or to the Moon, or if a benefic is in the first, dignified or exalted, and joined to the ruler of the first or the Moon; or the ruler of the first or the Moon joined to Jupiter or Venus in the first, tenth or seventh, the debt will be paid.

If Uranus, Saturn or Mars rules the eighth, seventh or second and afflicts the Moon or ruler of the first; the ruler of the eighth a malefic and in no reception of the ruler of the first or second, the money will be lost.

If the ruler of the seventh is in the eighth without mutual reception, or the Part of Fortune is afflicted in the first, seventh, or eighth, he is not able to pay the debt.

The ruler of the seventh or eighth retrograde, combust or peregrine, with no aspect to the benefics, the debtor is a cheat or dishonest; therefore little good can be expected, particularly if it is Neptune, Mars or Mercury, and badly aspected.

If the ruler of the seventh or eighth applies to the ruler of the second or to the Part of Fortune or its dispositor, he intends to defraud, and if the evil application is to the ruler of the first or the Moon, he has planned it and is determined not to pay.

The Part of Fortune always denotes money, whether in cash or bills; but property, whether in goods or land, houses, etc., is always shown by the ruler of the second or a planet there.

Will It Be Safe to Cash a Check, Etc.

It is safe to cash the check if the ruler of the first, second or the Part of Fortune is unafflicted, especially by the ruler of the seventh, eighth or the disposer of the Part of Fortune.

If the ruler of the seventh, eighth, first, second or the Part of Fortune is afflicted, or if the ruler of the first or second should happen to be ruler of the seventh or eighth, it is not safe to cash the check.

Shall I Return Safe from War?

The first, its ruler and the Moon signify the querent; the seventh and its ruler the enemy. If the figure is erected for a relative, the house of such relative may be taken for the Ascendant, and the opposite house for the enemy. Or it may be erected at the will of the querent for a relative as for any other person, by giving him the real Ascendant.

If Mars is weak in the figure, the querent will be fearful and probably be disgraced. The same is true if Uranus or Saturn is in the Ascendant or tenth house.

The South Node in the first or tenth is said to have a similar effect. The ruler of the first combust, retrograde, peregrine or cadent are all disastrous afflictions.

Saturn in conjunction with the ruler of the Ascendant shows fear and great misfortune. The square or conjunction of malefics denotes much evil. Saturn shows defeat and Mars wounds; and if he oppose either the Sun or Moon, there is danger of violent death; if it is applying to the conjunction, he will be killed on the spot.

Uranus gives explosions of magazines and guns. Mars in the Ascendant, especially if badly aspected, shows he will be dangerously wounded, and, if it is square or opposition to the Moon, it shows certain death.

The ruler of the seventh stronger than the ruler of the first and in opposition to the ruler of the first shows defeat, and, if it is a malefic, it denotes great dangers.

The ruler of the Ascendant or the Moon separating from the malefics and applying to the benefics is a sure sign of victory and safety. Mars well dignified in the tenth, or trine to the ruler of the ascendant or the Moon denotes victory; but if Mars squares or opposes the Sun or Moon there is great danger.

The ruler of the first joined to the North Node denotes courage and strength. In all aspects between the ruler of the seventh and first, that which is the strongest will be most victorious. If the ruler of the first and the Moon is free from affliction, the querent will return safely.

Evil planets in the eighth, he fears death. An evil planet ruling the first and a benefic in the Ascendant, then he will be found wounded but not killed.

Answers to Questions About War

The Ascendant and its ruler signify the person who asks the question. If the question is asked about another person, take the house and sign of the other person as the first house of the question, if about a blood relative take the third, for a child the fifth, for in-laws the ninth, for a friend the eleventh, for the spouse or just another person take the seventh for the first. The seventh house from their first would signify the enemy or foreign places.

If the ruler of the person's Ascendant or planet in that sign, the Moon or ruler of the seventh are conjunct in any angle, he is very sure to go.

If the rulers of the first and seventh are not conjunct but square or opposition from angles, he is sure to go. If there is a planet or planets in any angle, especially the first, translating the light from one planet to another, this shows activity in such a question.

If the aspect is square or opposition to the ruler of the first (the person), he may go, unless there is mutual reception at the same time. Mutual reception from angles mitigates the bad aspects.

If the heavier planets are in angular houses and the lighter planets in cadent and succedent, he is sure to go.

If the Moon, which is the fastest moving planet and also co-ruler of the question, is in the Ascendant or near the first house cusp and better aspected to that ruler and to the ruler of the twelfth or fourth than to the ruler of the seventh, sixth or eighth, the person will not serve in active warfare; if the chart signifies otherwise, he will serve the government in some manner at home, and if this aspect is to planets in the fourth or fifth houses, in some defense work or program.

If the Moon or any planet in the tenth is well aspected to the ruler of the first, this shows active contact with the government. If the Sun (natural ruler of power) is making no aspect to Saturn or Uranus (natural tenth and eleventh house rulers), there will be no active service away from the native country, especially across the seas.

If the person is already serving in the army or navy, especially across seas, when the question is asked, then consider the first, twelfth, seventh and eighth houses, whether it is a natal or a horary chart, to determine his safe return; use the rules for these houses to answer questions of such nature, using also the tenth for his honor, etc.

If the ruler of the Ascendant is combust, via combust, retrograde, peregrine or cadent, this denotes a disastrous end, disappointments or dissatisfaction to any undertaking.

If the rulers of the first and seventh do not make any aspect by application to each other but at the same time the Moon translates the light from the seventh to the first, it shows contact with foreign countries in such a question.

If there is a collection of light aspect between the two chief significators, the first and seventh, to a heavier planet, the person will probably enlist and later be called for active service. The time one will be called will be signified by the position of planets in the signs and houses, and the degrees they lack in making the aspect.

These rules are for horary questions, but the student will always find that they tie up in a radical way with the natal chart and the progressed planets. The progressed planets and the transiting planets stimulate the mind to ask such questions; therefore, there will be aspects as mentioned in these horary rules working in the natal chart when the question is asked, either by progression or by transit.

The astrologer should consult the person's natal chart in conjunction with all questions of such nature. This system, if followed, will be the means of avoiding many serious mistakes entering the advice we are able to give the person who asks such a question. If we do not believe that progression is necessary and certain and that transits do affect us, just as conditions do, just let us consider the condition of the world and people in it at any given period of history, and I rather think we will get the answer.

Whether Two Aries Will Fight

Observe the Ascendant, its ruler, the Moon and ruler of the seventh. If they are in conjunction in any angle, they will fight.

If the rulers of the first and seventh are not in conjunction but in square or opposition from angles, they will fight, or if there is any planet that translates the light of one to the other by square or opposition, there will be a fight provided there is no reception between them.

But if there are none of these aspects and a benefic or lighter planet applies to a heavier planet, there will be no serious fight or quarrel.

Has the Querent Public Enemies?

If the ruler of the first or the Moon afflicts the ruler of the seventh, the querent has public enemies. The ruler of the first in Gemini or in opposition to many planets, he has many public foes; the same is true if many planets are in the seventh. Their relation, condition and quality are known by the house they rule. If the bad aspects are applying, the enmity will increase, but if separating, it will decrease.

The number of enemies may be known by the number of planets afflicting the ruler of the first and the Moon as well as any planet that may happen to be in the Ascendant, and their appearance will be described by the planets situated in the signs at the time of the question. Investigate the person's description by the signs the planets occupy.

Of Theft Questions in General

The Ascendant and its ruler denote the querent; the seventh and its ruler, or a peregrine in the seventh or in any of the angles or in the second house, usually denotes the thief.

The second house, its ruler and the Moon denote and describe the stolen thing; wherever the ruler of the second is, usually shows where the thing is.

First find out if the thing is really stolen by the following rules. It is not stolen if the Moon is in the second or ruler of the cusp of the second house; if the Moon is going to a conjunction or parallel of the ruler of the seventh, it shows it is mislaid.

If the Moon is ruler of the first and in the fourth, if the ruler of the second is in the fourth or the ruler of the first is in the fourth or ruler of the second is in the second, especially if the Moon is in good aspect to the ruler of the seventh shows it was taken as a practical joke, etc.

If the Moon is ruler of the fifth and is parallel or conjunct the ruler of the seventh, shows the article is mislaid. The ruler of the seventh in the first or disposing of the Moon, or the ruler of the first or the Moon disposing of the ruler of the seventh, or Uranus or Mars in Cancer in cadent houses shows it is not stolen.

If neither the disposer of the Moon nor the ruler of the second has recently separated from the ruler of the sixth, the article or things are mislaid.

They are stolen if the Moon or ruler of the first or second or the Part of Fortune is in parallel or conjunction or in evil aspect to the significator of the thief, or if there is any bad aspect from a malefic planet or the ruler of the seventh to the ruler of the first or the Moon.

If Uranus, Saturn, or Mars is in the first, peregrine, they are stolen. The significator of the thief in any bad aspect to the dispositor of the Moon shows it is stolen.

To Find Out Who the Thief Is

He is probably one of the family if the ruler of the seventh is in the seventh or if the planet signifying the thief is in the first or seventh. The same is true if the Sun or Moon is in the first or in its own house, in good aspect or in mutual reception either in the first or seventh houses; if the ruler of the first and the thief's significator are in the same house or conjunct, especially in the second or fourth house, someone in the home is indicated; if in the fifth, a son or daughter; if in the fourth or sixth, a servant or roomer, or if the ruler of the sixth is in the second the same; but the thief will be a stranger if the ruler of the thief is in the third, ninth, eighth or twelfth house of the question.

If the thief is represented by the Sun it shows either the father or someone in authority or the son's wife; if the Sun is setting, a neighbor is shown. The Moon denotes the Mother or the daughter's husband. Neptune denotes a common thief or someone of disreputable character or one who drinks or peddles dope. Uranus denotes a friend, who may be visiting you or whom you may visit. Saturn denotes servants, the grandfather, a roomer or a stranger. Jupiter shows professors, religious cranks or professionals. Mars would denote a relative, either a brother, cousin, or perhaps a neighbor. Venus denotes a woman, the wife, a housekeeper, or someone who comes into the home occasionally to work, or a waitress. Mercury denotes a young person connected in some way with the family. If Mars and Mercury both denote the thief, they are common thieves and bad characters in general.

If you prove by the rules that the article is stolen and find the ruler of the seventh in the first, say it is one of the family; it could throw suspicion to the querent or owner of the stolen article. If this ruler is in the second, it would denote the wife or husband or maid-servant; in the third, a brother or sister, blood relative, companion, messenger or favorite servant; in the fourth, the father or some older person, the father's relative, roomer, janitor or gardener; in the fifth, a child, either the querent's or a niece or nephew, a charity person or one who dissipates; in the sixth, a servant, lodger, roomer, laborer, or sick person. The ruler of the seventh in the seventh shows an enemy or someone who has a spite against the querent, or some vile, evil person; in the eighth, a person who comes to the house occasionally to labor, nurse, or someone who has been befriended by the querent; in the ninth, a tramp, religious crank, or someone temporarily reduced to want and privation; in the tenth, someone who does not need to turn thief; in the eleventh, some friend or person of trust, or someone who has performed a service for the querent; in the twelfth, a beggar, a miserable mean person, or someone who is envious of the querent, or a professional thief, a slick, smooth one.

Uranus, Saturn, Jupiter, Mars and the Sun usually denote a male thief. Mercury as usual could be of either sex depending on its aspects and position. Saturn and Uranus show one older; Jupiter, Mars and the Sun show one younger; Mercury denotes the very young. Venus and the Moon show females. Neptune shows either sex depending, like Mercury, on its position and aspects.

If the angles of the chart when the question is asked are fixed signs or if the significator of the thief is in a fixed sign and in no aspect with any planet in the second, there is only one thief.

But more than one thief is indicated if you find many planets afflicting the ruler of the second and the Part of Fortune or the dispositor of the Part of Fortune; if the significators are in double-bodied signs or in sextile or trine with other planets and the Sun and Moon are in angles and in square aspect. If the thief's significator is in Cancer, Scorpio or Pisces, or the angles are movable signs, or the Moon is in a double-bodied sign and in the first house, more than one thief is indicated.

If the ruler of the thief is in a fixed sign, the thief or thieves are quite some distance away; in common signs, not far away; in cardinal signs, in the neighborhood. If the Moon is angular, it shows the thief to be at home.

If the Moon is in a succedent house, he is near his home; in a cadent house, he is a long way off. The ruler of the seventh in the first, the thief lives near the querent. The ruler of the seventh in the seventh shows that he is hiding in his own place.

Will the Stolen Article Be Recovered?

This is shown by the aspects the Sun and Moon make to each other and to the disposer of the Moon and the Moon's application to its dispositor.

If the Moon or ruler of the seventh is trine the ruler of the seventh or first, or the ruler of the second or Venus is in the first; if the Moon is in the tenth or second trine a planet in the tenth or second; if the Sun and Moon are trine or parallel each other; if the ruler of the second is in the eleventh, fourth, or first; if the Moon is parallel or conjunct Venus or Jupiter in the second; if the disposer of the Part of Fortune is in the first or second; or if the ruler of the first is in the seventh with the Part of Fortune, it will be found after much searching. The Sun and Moon in the tenth and the ruler of the first and second parallel, conjunct or trine each other shows sudden recovery. The Moon in the ninth parallel, conjunct, square, or opposition Neptune, Uranus, Saturn or Mars and any of these planets retrograde shows that the thief will bring back the stolen property.

If the significator of the thief is afflicted in the sixth, the thief will be sent to prison. The Moon in the eighth in conjunction with Mars shows he will be arrested. The Moon or ruler of the seventh parallel, conjunct Neptune, Saturn, Uranus or Mars or the South Node in any angle shows he will be arrested. The ruler of the thief Via combust or conjunction the Sun, he will probably die or be killed. The thief will be protected by a friend if the ruler of the seventh is in the eleventh in good aspect to Venus or Jupiter; in the third, by strangers; in the ninth, by his kindred; in the first, by partners in crime or by someone with whom he does business, such as those who receive stolen goods; in the tenth, he is in hiding; in the twelfth, he is protected by servants; in the second, by his wife or someone with whom he is living.

If you find that the querent will recover the stolen article or thing and wish to know the time of the recovery, observe the planets that denote recovery and see how many degrees they are from aspect to each other; then judge according to the rules given.

When the Sun and Moon aspect the ruler of the first or the significator is increasing in light and motion and located in fortunate parts of the chart, sudden recovery is shown.

When to Sell Large Cattle

The Ascendant, its ruler and the Moon denote the person who wishes to sell. The seventh house and its ruler denote the buyer unless otherwise designated.

The twelfth and its ruler denote the animal. The twelfth house shows large animals, the sixth house small animals and pets, etc.

It is best to sell when the rulers of the twelfth and seventh are in good aspect to each other or when the seventh house ruler and the ruler of the Ascendant are in good aspect.

A good price may be obtained when the ruler of the twelfth and the planets ruling the querent's second or first and seventh are in mutual reception or other good aspect to each other and especially if these rulers are in their dignities.

Something will be wrong with the animals if the South Node or a retrograde malefic planet is in the twelfth house; if they are in the seventh, no bargain will be made or the buyer will in some manner deceive the seller.

Eighth House Questions, such as Premiums, Retirement Money, Social Security, Pensions, Wills.

The eighth house is a very important house. Most of the text books do not stress this house, as they do not consider it of very much importance other than with reference to death, etc. But with Pluto, the ruler of Scorpio and the octave of Mars, some say the Moon, it should be considered as one of the important houses.

The eighth house rules taxes, premiums, retirement money or wages (Social Security), old age pensions, etc., as well as money through wills and legacies and financial relations with other countries. Pluto is in Leo and will be for some time. Leo is the second house from the fourth (Cancer), and always denotes money for the home, including what we spend because we wish to spend and also what we are forced to pay out.

The eighth house is the tenth from the eleventh in the natural zodiac; it is therefore the honor of the eleventh or what will be made public through legislation. Uranus, the ruler of Aquarius, is exalted in Scorpio, and the eleventh house is the fourth from the eighth or the end of eighth house affairs.

That is probably why there is so much trouble over wills and why death is connected with them. But now we will have questions to be answered in connection with the eighth house pertaining to pensions, retirement money, etc.; in other words, a person will not have to die in order for another person to gain. Gain will rather be under a plan conforming to the ideal of the brotherhood of man or distribution to the masses through groups. It will be good policy for the government, tenth house, to make these movements practical.

Questions relating to each of the eighth house affairs should be synthesized with the house pertaining to that particular issue, thing, or circumstance.

Pensions, premiums, retirement wages should be considered with the tenth and eleventh houses. The eighth house is other people's money and will show, when read correctly with the proper house, from what source it will be derived. The following rules will make things clearer and will be found useful.

Legacies and Questions Concerning a Sick Person's Will

This question should be answered at the exact time the sick person signs the will, if possible. But if the question is asked, "What will be the end of this person's will?" see if the Moon or the ruler of the first or eighth are in movable signs; this shows there will be a change made in the will later on. But we should find out if the sick person will recover. The Moon, the Ascendant, and the ruler of the Ascendant badly afflicted via combust or peregrine shows death and that the will would probably not be changed.

But if Mars rules the Ascendant or is in the first house and the Moon is in bad aspect to Mars, the will may be stolen. If Saturn or Uranus afflict in any way, the will may be changed. Jupiter and Venus well aspected show that the sick person will recover and probably destroy that will and make another.

Will the Querent Obtain the Expected Legacy?

The Ascendant, its ruler, and the Moon denote the person who asks the question, but in any question of this kind it is necessary to have the proper house for the quesited. If the querent expects the legacy from a parent, whichever it may be, we would consider the tenth or fourth, but, in a general way, it would be the tenth house, and the eleventh would denote the substance, etc.

However, if the question is asked about a father-in-law or mother-in-law, we would consider the fourth house, which would be the tenth from the seventh (the husband's or wife's house), and the fifth would denote the substance, etc.

Take the tenth or the fourth for the Ascendant of the wife's or husband's parent as the first house of the question. If the ruler of the Ascendant (querent) and the Moon, co-ruler, are strong, that is in their own houses or exalted and not badly aspected to Uranus, Saturn, Mars or the South Node, and the ruler of the tenth or fourth, depending on who it is, is in good aspect to the ruler of the first or if the Moon translates the light from the ruler of the person asked about to the ruler of the querent or is in any other good aspect, the querent will inherit or receive what is expected. But if the ruler of the eighth is in its fall or detriment, peregrine, or via combust, and Uranus, Saturn or Mars is in the eighth afflicting the ruler of the first (querent) or the ruler of the first in the eighth afflicted, the querent will not receive the expected legacy, etc.

Persons and Circumstances Obstructing Inheritance or Legacies

If a person has a claim to an estate and knows there is wealth or estate but does not receive it and wishes to know why he does not, we must observe the afflicting planets to find out who hinders.

The rulers of the first and eighth, and the sign and house they are in, will describe the person and show the cause of the querent not receiving his or her rights. If Mercury is ruler of the eighth and is in the ninth in square or opposition to the Part of Fortune, there will be a lawsuit involved. If Uranus, Saturn or Mars is ruler of the eighth and in the ninth and in these bad aspects to the Part of Fortune, it may be a kinsman or servant who hinders.

Go around the chart, considering all the signs by whatever afflicts the eighth or the Part of Fortune in the same way as above. Use the same rules as in the prevention of marriage given in this book to find out who hinders.

It will never be obtained if Saturn, Uranus, Mars or the South Node or any two of them are in the eighth, or if the ruler of the eighth or second is in its fall, detriment, peregrine or via combust.

Will the Wife's or Husband's Portion Be Obtained?

The Ascendant, its ruler and the Moon represent the one who asks the question. The seventh house represents the one enquired about; the eighth is his money, legacies, etc.

The quesited is well off and will leave money, etc. if any of the following rules apply: the ruler of the eighth well aspected by the Moon, Jupiter, Venus, the Sun, the Part of Fortune, or any of these planets in the eighth or ruling the eighth; if the Part of Fortune is in the second; the rulers of the eighth and second in each other's houses or well aspected to each other; if the ruler of the eighth or the Dragon's Head is in the eighth; if the ruler of the eighth disposes of the Part of Fortune in the eighth and is in good aspect to Venus or Jupiter; the Part of Fortune in the eighth in Leo or Aquarius; if either Mercury, Jupiter or Venus is in good aspect to the Part of Fortune; or if the ruler of the fourth or the ruler of the tenth is in any good aspect or in mutual reception with the ruler of the eighth from angles.

The legacy will be obtained if the ruler of the eighth is not afflicted by the malefics; if the ruler of the querent is in any good aspect to the ruler of the eighth, or if a benefic planet is in the eighth or the Moon co-ruler translates the light from the ruler of the eighth to the ruler of the first or second; or if the ruler of the second and eighth are in mutual reception. If any of the above rules apply, the person asked about will leave money and the husband or wife (depending on who asked the question) will receive it.

The legacy will not be obtained if the rulers of the first and second are square or opposition the ruler of the eighth; if the ruler of the eighth is retrograde, via combust or peregrine, very little will be obtained; if the chief rulers of the houses in question are afflicted by the malefics or to each other, there will be nothing of consequence left for the querent.

Sometimes there is evidence of gain, but by the time outstanding debts are settled, there will be little, if any, left. This will all be made clear by following the rules given for such questions.

In answering questions concerning group funds such as retirement wages, old age pensions, etc., the tenth and eleventh houses and their rulers will have to be considered with the eighth and probably can not be answered correctly without the translation and collection of light aspects. Such questions have originated since any of the text books we now have were published. I have answered a few with success by combining my rulers for legacies, etc. with the tenth and eleventh houses and using the translation and collection of light aspects.

Use the eleventh house to denote the end of all such eighth house questions, as the eleventh is fourth from the eighth and the eighth is tenth from the eleventh, counting the eleventh house as the first.

The eighth house would represent the honor or public house of the eleventh or things made public through legislation regarding group money. I find Pluto, Mars and the Moon very prominent in questions of this nature.

Will I Live with My Parents?

The Ascendant, its ruler and the Moon denote the querent, and if the cardinal signs occupy the angles, or the cadent houses; if the ruler of the first is in the seventh, or if the Moon is going into the eighth house, if the ruler of the first is in the third or ninth house signs, or afflicted by the rulers of the fourth or tenth, this shows that the querent will probably live with parents.

But if the ruler of the first is in any of the fixed signs, and especially in the first ten degrees of that sign and in the cadent houses, this shows there will be no removal from the place they are in when the question is asked.

Shall We Have a Death in the Family Soon?

Uranus or Saturn passing through the eighth, you will, that year. The ruler of the eighth, third, tenth or fourth heavily afflicted, then death is approaching the family.

But if none of these occur, then death is not likely to enter the family soon. The malefics coming from the ninth to the cusp of the eighth, then say death after many months.

Ninth House Questions

Of Carrying Insurance or Indemnity Policies

The Ascendant, its ruler and the Moon are for the person who asks the question. If the ruler of the first or the Moon is in any bad aspect to the ruler of the ninth or any planet in the ninth house sign; if the ruler of the seventh (people contacted) is in any bad aspect to the ruler of the first or ninth; and if the ruler of the seventh and ninth are malefics, there is not much hope of obtaining either.

It will be obtained if the rulers of the first, seventh, ninth and second houses are unafflicted and if these houses are neither occupied by nor have their cusps afflicted by the malefics. Money will always be advanced for the above if you find Jupiter or Venus or the Part of Fortune in the seventh or ninth houses, but if there are malefic planets in the second, seventh, ninth and the Moon, Venus or Mercury are not translating any light aspect between the ruler of the first and ninth or between the ruler of the second and first, or making any good aspect to the disposer of the Part of Fortune, the person will not be able to afford insurance, etc.

The ninth house relates to insurance companies, indemnity policies, and to some extent to the value of wills and premiums (Scorpio) as Sagittarius is the second from the eighth.

Of the Success of Books, Etc.

This question may be answered by either setting up a chart for the time a book was started, for the time of its publication, or for whenever the author wishes to know about it.

For the best time to publish a book, I would suggest an election chart which is made to tie up with the natal chart as instructed in the rules given in this book. The production of a book is always signified by the second house, its ruler and planets in the second. If Mercury (natural third and sixth house ruler) and the Part of Fortune are in the ninth or if Mercury rules the ninth house cusp; if Mercury is dignified and well aspected to or by the rulers of the fourth, eighth, or twelfth houses; if Mercury is in its own house and sign, oriental the Sun and making a good aspect to the ruler of the ninth, you may be sure it will prosper.

Success is almost sure, when good planets are in the ninth and trine Mercury in the first, or when Mercury is in the ninth and well aspected by benefic planets in the Ascendant.

Do not expect success if Mercury or the ruler of the ninth is in the sixth or twelfth and badly afflicted; if Saturn or Mars is in the ninth and most of the planets are under the earth, and if any of them afflicts the ninth or its ruler. This will show many hindrances.

The planets that Mercury afflicts will show who hinders, and also those that afflict the ninth house rulers. It is well to have the Moon and Mercury making as many good aspects as possible, for this will show the book, etc. to be a successful business venture.

Of Profit Through Science and Higher Education

The ruler of the first and ninth in parallel or conjunction, sextile or trine, and applying to each other from angles or from a succedent house; Venus, Jupiter or the North Node in the ninth house, and Venus and Jupiter in signs of their dignity in good aspect to the Ascendant or planets in the Ascendant; the Moon in the second or ruling that cusp in sextile to the ninth house or its ruler, especially if the sign Aquarius is on the ninth house cusp; and the planet Uranus well aspected by the ruler of the first or to the cusp of the first, ninth or tenth houses—this shows much pleasure and profit in the above affairs.

If you do not find any of the above in the chart, and there should be a square or opposition between the ruler of the first and ninth, or if the Dragon's Tail, Neptune, Saturn, Uranus or Mars is in the first or ninth afflicting the rulers of these houses or the Moon afflicting these malefics, do not expect to gain through science, college or higher education because there will be no gain, and the chart will denote why.

Will the Clergyman or Professor Obtain the Appointment?

The Ascendant, its ruler and the Moon signifies the clergyman or whoever asks the question, and the ninth house the appointment or whatever he is seeking. The tenth house is the salary he may expect if he gets the appointment.

If the Moon or the ruler of the first is in good aspect to the ruler of the ninth, or if the Moon is translating the light aspect from the ruler of the first to the ruler of the ninth; if the ruler of the first or the Moon is in the ninth or the first; if the ruler of the ninth and the first are in mutual reception; if the ruler of the first or the Moon is in parallel or other good aspect to the Sun and Jupiter in the first or ninth; if the ruler of the first, ninth or the Moon are aspected to each other, even from a square or opposition mutual reception aspect, it shows gain, though in the last instance it will come after much labor and hindrance.

If the ruler of the first separates from any good aspect to the ruler of the ninth and a minor planet aspects first the ninth and then the ruler of the first or the Ascendant, there will be gain by means of a person described by this planet.

There will be no gain if the ruler of the first is retrograde, via combust, combust, or if the Moon is in bad aspect to the malefic planets, or if the rulers of the twelfth, third or sixth are in bad aspect to the ruler of the ninth house cusp.

If a malefic is in the ninth or its ruler is retrograde, there is hindrance and uneasiness of mind. Malefics in either the first or ninth, afflicting their rulers, or the Moon afflicting either of these planets, there will be trouble and disappointment.

The cause of the above will be shown by the planet that makes the malefic aspect and the sign and house the ruler or malefic is in, such as in the third a relative or neighbor; in the eleventh a friend; in the twelfth secret things; in the tenth he is unpopular; in the ninth religious relations or perhaps his doctrine is not to their liking or belief; in the seventh or fifth he is either contentious, immoral or in some way improper; if in the sixth health, want of activity or some unforeseen misfortune; in the second the salary does not satisfy.

Tenth House Questions

When Shall I Obtain a Situation?

The Ascendant, its ruler, and the Moon denote the person asking the question. When the ruler of the first and the ruler of the tenth or a planet in the tenth make a parallel or good aspect to each other, the person will obtain the situation, and the degrees between these rulers will show when it will be obtained. Give for every degree a day, week, etc., according to the position in angular, succedent, or cadent houses in movable, fixed or cardinal signs.

If the above rules do not apply satisfactorily, see when the Sun and the ruler of the first make a good aspect; this will show the time.

The Moon translating the light from the ruler of the first to the ruler of the tenth would be favorable. The Moon, co-ruler of the querent, in the tenth, or parallel, conjunction, sextile or trine the ruler of the tenth, Venus, Jupiter or the Sun would bring a position of eminence and security. The above aspects to these planets gives honor and dignity.

The career or business for which the person is best fitted is shown by the sign on the tenth house cusp and the planet in the sign, also the aspects to the Sun, its sign and position. This will be the line of least resistance.

If Mercury should rule, it produces writers, teachers, merchants and bankers.

Venus, musicians, artists, makers of wearing apparel, perfumers, shop keepers.

Jupiter, a professional career, orators, members of the legislature, judges, bishops.

Saturn, positions of responsibility with land and property.

Uranus, science, engineering, government or civil officials.

Mars, surgeons, dentists, soldiers, sailors.

Neptune, work of an inspirational nature, psyches, etc., the motion picture industry and allied arts.

But if the querent asks the question, take the ruler of the first and the Moon for the querent, the ruler of the tenth and fifth as well as planets in the tenth, for the best trade or situation to follow. If the majority of the planets that rule these house cusps or that are in these houses are in water signs, the person would be best as a druggist or at work in drug stores, or in any trade that has to do with liquids, herbs or drugs.

If they are in fire signs, it would denote a chemist, surgeon, physician, glassware or steel worker; if in air signs, a lawyer, accountant, surveyor, clerk, astronomer or astrologer, painter, designer, printer, bookseller, or any business not too sedentary and chiefly in the retail trade; in earth signs, a gardener or grower, a carpenter, bricklayer or mason, an agriculturist, or any calling connected with the earth or substances produced from it.

Shall I Prosper in Business?

If the person is in business at the time the question is asked, he will prosper if the Moon and rulers of the first and tenth are in good aspect with each other, and also if the Part of Fortune, Jupiter, Venus or the North Node is in the tenth. The rulers of the tenth, eleventh, and first in parallel or good aspect with each other, he will prosper in the business.

But if the ruler of the first, tenth, the Sun and Moon are in bad aspect, it will prove unfortunate. Losses, etc. are indicated if the South Node, Saturn, Mars, Neptune or Uranus are either in the tenth and afflicted, or afflicting the eleventh cusp or its ruler.

Shall I Obtain this Situation?

If the ruler of the first or the Moon is in the tenth and well aspected, or the ruler of the tenth or the Sun is in the first, strong and well aspected; the Moon in good aspect to the ruler of the first or translating the light from the ruler of the first to the ruler of the tenth; the ruler of the tenth, a fortunate planet and in the tenth well aspected; the ruler of the first or tenth parallel, conjunction or in other good aspect to the North Node, the Sun, Jupiter or Venus in the tenth or first; the ruler of the tenth and the ruler of the first in mutual reception; exalted planets in the first or tenth and the Moon in good aspect to either; the Moon separating from the ruler of the first by parallel, conjunction or other good aspect and applying to the tenth or planets in the tenth.

If Saturn, Neptune, Uranus or Mars is strong in the first and in conjunction, parallel or good aspect to the ruler of the tenth, the position may be gained even though the last rule indicates some delay. It will not be obtained if two or more of the above rules are not found.

Expect to be disappointed if any of the following rules apply: if Uranus, Neptune, Saturn, Mars or the South Node are in the tenth or afflict the rulers of the first and tenth, or if the Moon afflicts any of the above, the querent will be hindered from contacting the person he is to solicit; if the ruler of the tenth is in bad aspect to the Sun, Moon or ruler of the first, Mars or the ruler of the tenth in its detriment or fall or in the via combust way, there will be disappointment in obtaining the position.

Shall I Continue in My Present Situation?

You will stay if the ruler of the first and tenth are parallel, conjunction, or other good aspect and if the most ponderous planet of the two is in any angle but the fourth; if the Moon is parallel or conjunct the ruler of the tenth in the tenth, or if the ruler of the first or the Moon is parallel, conjunction or in other good aspect to the tenth and its ruler or a planet in the tenth house cusp.

If the ruler of the first is in good aspect to Jupiter, Venus or the North Node in the tenth and no evil aspect is found to Neptune, Uranus, Saturn, Mars or the South Node, it will be long before he leaves.

Shall I Leave My Present Situation?

You will be sure to leave if two or more of the following rules apply: if the Moon or ruler of the first is in bad aspect to the ruler of the tenth or a planet in the tenth house cusp, or if the Sun is badly aspected; if the ruler of the first or the Moon is separating from the ruler of the tenth and applying to Neptune, Uranus, Saturn, Mars or the South Node, you will be sure to leave.

If the rulers of the tenth and first are in bad aspect and the most ponderous planets are in the fourth; if the Moon or ruler of the fourth is in Aries, Cancer, Libra or Capricorn in the fourth or if the Moon is in Capricorn and afflicted or void of course and the ruler of the first is afflicted, you will lose your position and will probably leave when the disposer of the ruler of the first, tenth or Moon comes to a conjunction with the Sun, turns retrograde or leaves the sign they are in when the question was asked.

See when the ruler of the tenth or planet in the tenth leaves the sign it is in; about that time you will leave.

What Will Be the Cause of Leaving?

If the ruler of the first or the Moon is in bad aspect with any planet, and that planet is parallel, conjunct or in any good aspect with either the tenth house ruler or the Sun, harm will come from such persons as are described by the planets that are in good aspect to the Sun or ruler of the tenth.

If the ruler of the first is retrograde or combust the Sun or in the via combust way, you have yourself to blame and are the cause of your leaving.

Of the Success of a Petition to Any Person in Power

The first house and its ruler signify the petitioner; the fifth, its ruler and the Moon signify the petition.

The tenth, its ruler and the Sun denote the person to whom the petition is directed or with whom entrusted.

The petition will be successful if the ruler of the first, the Moon and the Ascendant are well aspected by any of the benefics and to the tenth house cusp and its ruler; if the ruler of the fifth or the Moon is in the tenth or first, dignified and well aspected; if Jupiter, Venus or the Sun rules the tenth cusp; if the fortunate planets are angular and the malefics cadent. If the Moon is in the tenth, strong and in good aspect to the Sun, or if the ruler of the tenth is in good aspect to any planet in the tenth.

The petition will be unsuccessful if the ruler of the first, fifth or the Moon is afflicted by the ruler of the fourth, eighth, tenth or twelfth, or if the ruler of the fifth afflicts, the petition was not properly presented; if the Moon afflicts, the petition is probably erroneous in some of its clauses.

Whether an Exile Will Be Restored

The Ascendant, its ruler and the Moon denote the person, officer, nobleman, gentleman, etc.

If the ruler of the first is conjunct (except it be the Sun) the ruler of the tenth or in aspect with the tenth house cusp; if the Moon is conjunct a fortunate planet in the first or tenth or the Moon translates the light from the ruler of the first to the ruler of the tenth; if the ruler of the tenth is a lighter planet than the ruler of the first; if the ruler of the first is dignified and parallel, sextile or trine to a planet in mutual reception, the person will be restored to his former place or residence, office or government.

But he will never be restored if the Moon is afflicted in the third or ninth.

But if the Moon is well aspected in the third or ninth then he may try to gain office or be restored or gain popularity in another place.

The time he will be restored should be judged when the planets come in good aspect to each other according to their degrees of distance apart.

If the ruler of the first and tenth are separating from any aspect to each other or the Moon or if the ruler of the tenth is afflicted in the first, tenth, seventh or fourth, the person will never be restored.

Eleventh House Questions, Including Group Legislation, Reforming of Matrimonial Laws, New Inventions, Adjustment of Relationships

The eleventh house is a most important house and answers questions pertaining to all kinds of circumstances and events having to do with groups.

The eleventh house is the fifth from the seventh counting the seventh as the first of any seventh house question, and the fifth from the third. These three houses have to do with relationship. Eleventh house is unbonded relationship.

This eleventh house will have much to do with reforming or changing of all so-called legal laws or those that are at present considered legal. Uranus is called the planet of the meeting and the parting of the affinities; Uranus badly aspected brings more divorces and broken engagements than any other planet.

It is my opinion when the planet Neptune enters Libra, the seventh house sign, and when Uranus enters Gemini, the third house sign, that all circumstances regarding relationship will be entirely changed and revised, and that new laws regarding marriage and divorce will be adopted. Reforms of all kinds will be made regarding these houses and questions pertaining to them.

Aquarius, Gemini, and Virgo are human signs, and Libra is the meeting place or the sign of balance. Gemini is the sign of the twins, Virgo of the Virgin, and Aquarius of the regenerated man.

Neptune in Libra, the balance or scales, will eventually bring some kind of balance or decent state of marriage. Neptune is the spiritual ruler of Pisces, twelfth house affairs. Neptune is democratic in nature and will increase or help the power of the people.

The eleventh house is the fourth from the eighth; therefore it is the end of wills, legacies and all that the eighth house signifies. When did we ever hear of a will or legacy that wasn't disputed or questioned in some way?

The eighth is the second from the seventh, so Uranus will change all these affairs in the near future. Drastic changes along all lines will eventually materialize; all beliefs and opinions, especially traditions, will have to go.

Uranus' cycle is seven years in a sign, we know that every seven years we have a change on all planes of consciousness. One of the interpretations of the eleventh house, Aquarius concerns friends, hopes and wishes.

The kind of friends we have will depend on the kind of friend we are; what we hope for and wish for will depend on our mental ability to choose what is best for us within ourselves. Aquarius, being the eleventh sign and eleventh period, refers to the rise in consciousness far in advance to our present day period, so there will be new laws (ninth house) legislated (eleventh house).

The eleventh house, its ruler and planets in this house have to do with all eleventh house questions. The first house, its ruler and planets in the first, and the Moon denote the querent.

If Uranus rules or is in the eleventh house and the Sun, Moon, Venus or Mercury is parallel, conjunct, sextile or trine Uranus, a person will prosper in all eleventh house questions and have many friends, making them helpful, sincere, original and clever.

Shall I Obtain My Hope, Wish or Whatever Pertains to Eleventh House Affairs?

If the Moon is in any good aspect to Venus, the Sun, Mercury or Uranus, or if the Moon and any of these planets is in mutual reception, it will be obtained.

But if the receiver of the Moon is a malefic planet or badly aspected, it shows that after the thing is gained, evil will follow.

The ruler or co-ruler of the first and eleventh houses in good aspect with each other or the Moon, or in mutual reception; the ruler of the first well aspected in the eleventh or the ruler of the eleventh in any good aspect to the first or in the Ascendant; the ruler of the eleventh in any angle, well aspected, and in good aspect to the ruler of the first; the ruler of the first in mutual reception with the Moon shows that the querent will receive his desires, hopes and wishes, or whatever the eleventh house denotes.

If the Moon and the ruler of the Ascendant apply to a good aspect of the Part of Fortune and the planets Venus or Jupiter are not cadent, expect the thing inquired about to materialize.

If the ruler of the eleventh is a fortunate planet and applies to the ruler of the first by evil aspect, it may be obtained with difficulty.

There will be no gain through eleventh house affairs if the Moon is not well aspected to the ruler of the eleventh, and if the benefic planets or the North Node do not occupy the eleventh house.

If the rulers are in bad aspect to each other, via combusta, combust, retrograde, cadent, void of course, or with malefic fixed stars, it will not be obtained.

What Kind of a Person Will Prove to Be My Best Friend?

The ruler of the Ascendant or the Moon in parallel, conjunction, trine or sextile to planets in the eleventh house brings friends of the nature of the sign and planets in the eleventh.

Air signs give intellectual friends, fire signs give impulsive and enthusiastic friends, earth signs give obstinate and sometimes wayward or practical friends, water signs give emotional, erratic and sensual friends.

Venus and Mercury in the eleventh bring many friends who are artistic and intellectual, especially if they are in good aspect with Jupiter and Venus; the Moon gives friendship with women.

If the Sun or Moon is square or opposition with Saturn, Mars or Uranus, a person does not make friends easily, especially with the opposite sex.

The masculine planets are the Sun, Mars, Jupiter, Saturn and

Uranus. The feminine planets are the Moon, Venus, Neptune and sometimes Mercury, depending on Mercury's sign.

The person who is our best friend, male or female, that we can depend on and trust, is described by the planet or planets in the eleventh house and the sign in which they are placed.

Is this Person a Friend to Me?

The Ascendant, its ruler and the Moon denote the person who asks the question. The eleventh house and its ruler denote the friend.

The friend is sincere if there is any good aspect between the ruler or co-ruler of the first and eleventh, or mutual reception between these rulers.

If the Moon is in any good aspect to the ruler of the eleventh, if good planets or the North Node is in the eleventh, and if the planets in the eleventh or its ruler make any good aspect to the ruler of the second, there is gain through friends.

The friend is not sincere if the South Node is there; if the ruler of the first or the Moon is in any bad aspect to the ruler of the eleventh or to Neptune, Uranus, Saturn or Mars; or if Jupiter or Venus is in any bad aspect to this ruler.

The ruler of the eleventh in the twelfth with the South Node, they are deceitful. Mercury in the eleventh and afflicted gives changeable and deceitful friends.

Good and bad planets make much difference in these questions. Malefics always cause things that are disagreeable no matter how well aspected they are, while the benefics, however badly aspected they are, never cause a very great degree of harm.

Application denotes reconciliation, if the aspect applying is good, or a renewing of differences if the aspect is evil.

Planets separating from each other show a breaking of attachments if the aspect was good, or if it has been evil, it denotes contempt or indifference, and, if no good aspect follows to a benefic planet, the friendship will never be renewed.

Twelfth House Questions, Including Circumstances Pertaining to Enforced Labor Conditions, Advanced Therapeutic Procedures Combining Medical and Metaphysical Methods.

This is another house that is not given its proper attention. Like all the houses from the seventh to the first, this is one of the houses to receive future recognition because it is the house of enforced labor, social outcasts or self-imposed isolation.

This will all be improved in the future; all twelfth house matters will improve. Depressed and discouraged people will through help and education be taught that they do not have to be subservient to the whims of others. They will no longer ignorantly and blindly obey their lords and masters. Neptune, ruler of Pisces, has been slowly and gradually bringing light out of darkness.

The concealing and keeping of truths for specially privileged people is a thing of the past. Pisces and the twelfth house are enforced ignorance and labor. Virgo is the outcome of these enforcements, the enlightenment and truth for all, not for a specially privileged few.

The unlucky person, thief, beggar, criminal, or any person who lives from charity (twelfth house) is a victim of circumstance. When truth, sanity and law (Saturn) are evenly distributed, there will be fewer of these victims.

No wonder the twelfth house and the sign Pisces is spoken of as the "poor fish and dumb, driven cattle."

This house is called the house of secret enemies; this means some one or some thing is inharmonious.

Disease, sickness and ignorance are the only real enemies because these things limit and confine us so that we do not understand

and think. We do not need so many prisons, but more schools and hospitals where the downtrodden and ignorant people will be educated and helped.

The more people that receive these things in their true light, the less we will need reforms and prisons.

The teaching of chemistry, physiology and astrology will eventually do away with crime.

All questions pertaining to hospitals, prisons, asylums, and private enemies belong to the twelfth house.

Questions About Private Enemies

When a person knows or suspects that he has private enemies and fears the effect of their malice, etc., take the ruler of the first and the Moon to signify the person who asks the question; the ruler of the twelfth or the planet afflicted in the twelfth to describe the enemy.

The planet ruling the twelfth or the planet afflicting the ruler of the first will usually describe the general appearance of the enemy. See what planet rules the twelfth cusp; if it is Neptune, Saturn, Mars or Mercury and in bad aspect to the ruler of the first, or the Sun and the Moon is in bad aspect to these planets, it denotes enemies or the enemy described by that planet and by the sign in which it or they happen to be.

The house in which this planet is placed will reveal, at least in part, the cause and quality of the enmity as well as other peculiarities concerning the affair.

The malefics in the twelfth or seventh denote many enemies; also, if the ruler of the first is badly aspected in the seventh or twelfth or either of their rulers is in the first, there are enemies.

If the ruler of the twelfth is in the third and is in bad aspect to the Moon or ruler of the first, they are blood relatives or neighbors, especially if the ruler of the third is otherwise afflicted.

If in the fourth it would be the father; in the fifth, children, some visitor, or someone of unbonded relationship; in the sixth or joined to its ruler, servants, an uncle or aunt (if the ruler of the sixth is in the twelfth, afflicted, the aunt or uncle would be sickly or insane); if the ruler of the twelfth afflicts the first from the seventh, it could be the wife or husband, partner or any person with whom we do business; in the eighth, it would be enemies through wills, legacies, etc.; in the ninth, through in-laws, lawyers, preachers, etc.; in the tenth or with the tenth house ruler the enemy is in the service of some so-called respectable person, and, if he is strong, it will be well not to interfere with him. The ruler of the twelfth in the eleventh is a foe in the guise of a friend.

The querent may also expect evil influence from that house in which the South Node is placed, especially if the disposer of the South Node is in any bad aspect to either the ruler of the first, or the Moon applies to a bad aspect of either.

How Much Power Do They Possess?

If the ruler of the twelfth is a major planet and dignified, they are powerful and therefore dangerous.

If the ruler of the first is angular, better dignified, or well aspected by the benefics than the ruler of the twelfth, the querent will overcome his enemies.

If the ruler of the twelfth and the ruler of the first are the same planet and the Moon is making a bad aspect to this planet, the querent is his own worst enemy and is the cause of any enemies he makes. At the same time, if an evil planet is in the twelfth, he has formed an evil connection and will reap discontent and sorrow from his own folly.

There Are No Private Enemies

If the ruler of the first or the Moon is well aspected, or if Jupiter or Venus is in the twelfth and not afflicted; if the first, its ruler, and the Moon are well placed with no bad aspects to the malefic planets, he has no private enemies. If the ruler of the eleventh is stronger than the ruler of the seventh or twelfth, then friends will be more powerful than enemies.

If the planet or planets signifying enemies is peregrine, retrograde, or via combust, the enemies are malicious, mean characters.

Of Imprisonment or Banishment, Persons Transported or in Any Way Exiled

The ruler of the first and the Moon denote the person that is in prison or banished, etc., whoever it may be—a parent, relation, neighbor, friend or anyone in the public light.

Freedom is denoted by the ruler of the first or the Moon being swift and unafflicted, especially if the ruler of the twelfth is in a movable sign and in good aspect to a fortunate planet; also, if the ruler of the twelfth is stronger than the ruler of the seventh, third or ninth; if the ruler of the first or the Moon separates from the ruler of the fourth and immediately applies to a fortunate planet.

A long confinement is shown if the ruler of the first or the Moon is in a fixed sign in a cadent house; if the ruler of the first is in the fourth, sixth, eighth or twelfth, via combusta or retrograde; if the ruler of the first is in bad aspect to Neptune, Uranus, Saturn or Mars or if the ruler of the first is under the Sun's beams; if the ruler of the twelfth afflicts Uranus, Neptune, Saturn or Mars and either of these malefics is the ruler of the eighth, the person will die in prison.

A fixed sign on the first, its ruler in the twelfth, and a heavier planet angular shows long confinement or imprisonment.

If the ruler of the first and twelfth is the same planet, it denotes lasting misfortunes unless it is well dignified and aspected.

If the ruler of the first is in a cadent house in Scorpio or Aquarius, the same is shown. The Moon or the Sun in opposition to Saturn, Uranus, Neptune or Mars or the Moon or ruler of the first near any fixed violent star, especially Caput Algol, denotes the end through violent death or that he will die in prison or be executed.

The time of release, if release is indicated, may be known by observing the degree of distance between the ruler of the twelfth and the benefics or between the good aspects of the Sun and the ruler of the twelfth, or the degree between the applying planets and whether these planets are in cardinal, fixed or common signs, according to the measure of time. The last aspect the Moon makes, good or bad, will determine the outcome of any question.

Elections

In the use of elections the questioner may ascertain with certainty the best time to start any enterprise he wishes to be successful.

When the house cusp or planet in a particular house is afflicted in the natal chart, it is difficult many times for affairs pertaining to that house to prove successful.

However, it is possible and practical to obtain a favorable time for all affairs. This is called making an election.

If the following rules are observed and used, the astrologer or student may make any election chart for any specific venture and carry it through to a successful conclusion.

The first house tells the success of any enterprise; therefore, we will see that the Moon is well aspected to the planet under which the person was born and have the same sign rising in this election chart that was rising at birth, providing it is not afflicted by a malefic. If we are making an election for anything of long duration, place Taurus, Scorpio, Leo or Aquarius on the cusp of the first house.

In elections for second house affairs, have the Moon well aspected to the planet that was ruler of the rising sign in the natal chart and also to the planet Jupiter. Let either of these planets be in the second house of the election chart and well aspected.

In elections for third house affairs, have the planet under which the person was born in good aspect with the Moon and the Moon's dispositor.

If possible, have planets in the third house which are well aspected to the third cusp of the natal chart, but do not let these rulers be the rulers of the sixth, eighth or twelfth houses.

If the election is for a journey, consider the purpose of the trip; let the ruler of that for which you take the journey be well aspected and the Moon well aspected to the ruler of that cusp. If the journey is for business purposes, see that the tenth cusp of the election chart is well fortified; if for pleasure, consider the fifth house and so on for each house, depending on the purpose of the trip.

If possible have the Part of Fortune in the third house of the election chart. Never place Mars in the third house for any journey, no matter how well aspected it is, unless it was in the third house at birth and well aspected. Mars is evil for journeys and brings danger of robbery and accident. It is well to have the Moon increasing in light for journeys.

In elections for fourth house affairs, have the planet that was ruler of the fourth house at birth in the fourth or ruling the cusp of the fourth in the election chart. Have the Moon applying to a good aspect. The Part of Fortune here improves all fourth house questions.

In elections for fifth house questions, have the ruler of the fifth house of the natal chart placed in the second house of the election chart, and let Jupiter and Venus be well aspected to the cusp of the fifth house. Be careful not to afflict the first house and its ruler, and have these rulers better aspected than the ruler of or planets in the seventh house.

In elections for sixth house affairs, have the Moon well aspected to the sixth house or in the sixth house in the sign of Taurus,

Gemini, or Capricorn; also have the ruler of the second house of the natal chart in the sixth house of the election chart in good aspect to the first. Be sure to have no combust planets in the sixth house of the election chart.

In elections for seventh house affairs, have the ruler of the first and the Moon well aspected to the ruler of seventh. These planets must not be in any affliction to Uranus, Neptune, Saturn, Mars or the South Node or by the Moon. Have Aquarius or Leo on the cusp of the first house of the election chart.

In elections for eighth house affairs, have the ruler of the first in the natal chart and the Moon on the day of the election well aspected. Have the ruler of the first or planet in the first house of the election chart in good aspect to the planet Saturn; also have the Moon applying to a good aspect of Saturn.

In elections for ninth house affairs, have the ruler of the ninth in the natal chart and the ruler of the ninth house in the election chart free from affliction. Consider the purpose of the election, and have the planets ruling this particular venture in the ninth house of the election chart and well aspected.

If Aquarius could be placed on this cusp, and Uranus, ruler of Aquarius, in good aspect to the ruler of the cusp of the first house of the natal chart or to the ninth or tenth houses, it would be a good election.

In elections for tenth house affairs, have the cusp of the tenth house in the natal chart, the cusp of the first house of the election chart, and the ruler of the tenth and first in good aspect to each other; have the Moon applying to a good aspect of either or both. Also consider the ruler of the eleventh house, as the eleventh reveals the fruits of the tenth or indicates the gain to be derived from tenth house affairs.

In elections for eleventh house affairs, have Venus or Jupiter in the eleventh or ruling the sign on the cusp of the eleventh in the election chart and in good aspect to the ruler of the natal chart.

In elections for all twelfth house affairs, have the ruler of the first in the election chart and the Moon well aspected to the ruler of the twelfth or to planets in the twelfth house of the birth chart.

The student will find a specimen chart illustrating an election made for a journey for a person who had an afflicted third house at birth.

This chart proves that a fortunate time can be obtained for any undertaking by selecting a time in the current ephemeris when it is favorable to undertake it. All charts will prove successful and beneficial if erected according to the rules given for them.

Election for a Journey

The chart shown is an election chart made for a woman living in Los Angeles who wished to go east, dispose of her home and furniture, and return to Los Angeles for permanent residence. This election was made for March 30, 1941 at 7:35 a.m. True Local Mean Time; a Sun day and a Mercury hour.

The following is the correct procedure (and rules) for any election chart. First always consider the person's natal chart. This woman had Virgo on the eastern horizon of her natal chart. The planet Mercury is her ruler. She had Scorpio on her third house cusp with Mars in Scorpio afflicted.

She had been hindered from making the trip at different times so we decided to make an election for the best time for her.

Following the rules given for election charts we must have the Moon of the election chart in good aspect to the planet Mercury, the woman's ruler, as this is a third house affair (journey). We wish to have the ruler of the first and the third well aspected to each other, and the Moon in good aspect to the Part of Fortune or to the dispositor of the Part of Fortune. Moreover we wish to have the Moon making as many good aspects as possible as it is co-ruler of health, business, money, etc. We must also have the houses pertaining to these affairs and their rulers well aspected.

A chart for March 30, 1941 at 7:35 a.m. is splendid and gives 15 Taurus 20 on the eastern horizon with the Moon, Saturn, Jupiter and Uranus rising. Venus, ruler of Taurus (woman) and also of her sixth house cusp (her health) is conjunct the Sun in Aries and sextile the Part of Fortune in the second house of her money. Mercury, ruler of Gemini on the second cusp, is square the Part of Fortune, but Mercury is in Jupiter's sign elevated above the Part of Fortune in her eleventh house of hopes and wishes and thus mitigates this square to some degree. The Moon, co-ruler of the chart and ruler of Cancer and the third and fourth house cusps (her journey, home and end of the matter) is exalted in Taurus and is coming to a sextile of Mercury, the woman's ruler (Mercury, ruler of Virgo), and to a conjunction and parallel of Saturn, a conjunction of Jupiter and Uranus, and a trine to Neptune and to Mars. Mars was in her natal third house. Mercury rules the intercepted sign in the fifth house and the sign Gemini on the second house cusp. Mercury is sextile Saturn, Jupiter and Uranus. Saturn, ruler of the ninth and tenth houses, shows she will have the opportunity to profit by what these houses signify.

Jupiter is ruler of intercepted Pisces in the eleventh house (friends, hopes and wishes) and also of the eighth house cusp (other people's money). Mars is exalted in Capricorn and conjunct the tenth house cusp (business) and rules the seventh house cusp (where she is going and those she will contact in a business way). The last aspect the Moon makes is a trine to Mars which shows gain for her in all the affairs pertaining to this chart.

The woman left Los Angeles at 7:35 a.m. on March 30, 1941, reached her destination, had a splendid time socially (the Moon trine Neptune in the fifth house and sextile Mercury, ruler of the intercepted sign in the fifth house-pleasure), sold her home and returned to Los Angeles, bringing two vans of antique furniture with her. The Moon rules the third and fourth house cusps (the journey and the home), and Taurus with Jupiter and Saturn on the first cusp and Uranus in the first rules antique furniture.

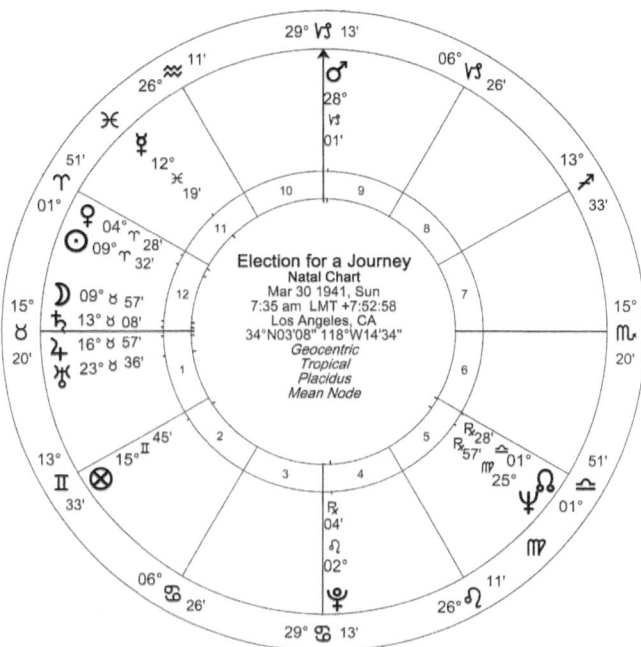

She was in better health than when she left on the trip; Venus, ruler of the sixth house, her health, is in the twelfth in the sign Aries; and Mars, ruler of Aries, disposes of the planet Venus. The Moon is translating the light from Saturn to Jupiter and then to Uranus and trine Mars. This is a Sun day and a Mercury hour. The Sun rules business, honor, etc. and Mercury rules journeys, contracts, paper money, etc. Pluto on the cusp of the fifth house shows pleasure derived from the journey because the first house is ruled by Venus, and Venus is trine Pluto, and the first house is the ninth house from the fifth.

The fixed signs Taurus and Scorpio on the cusps of the first and seventh show hindrance of long standing in making trips in the past, but the cardinal sign Cancer on the third and fourth cusps, ruled by the Moon, and the Moon sextile Mercury and conjunction Uranus, natural travel planets, releases these hindrances. The Moon's last aspect is a trine to Mars, ruler of the seventh house of where she is going; Mars is exalted in the ninth where formerly it was afflicted in the third. Both the Moon and Mars are exalted, showing the success of this election chart.

It is never well to begin any enterprise when the Moon is going to join or make any aspect to a retrograde planet. It will prove disappointing. Also, never have Jupiter under the Sun's beams when you wish to transact any business, for it is sure to end in disappointment.

The first twelve hours of the New Moon are not as good for the beginning of any venture as the following twelve hours. It is better to begin an enterprise three days after the new Moon, providing the Moon is well placed and well aspected. If one wishes to sell anything, try to do so when the Moon is in her first quarter and going to the full. But if one wishes to buy something, it is best to do so when the Moon is in its full and going to her last quarter.

The best book to use for election charts is *The Rulership Book* by Rex E. Bills. It gives the planets that rule over all the different affairs of life. Election charts used in this way are successful. Try them and prove to yourself that there is a time best suited for everything pertaining to the twelve houses or departments of life.

www.ingramcontent.com/pod-product-compliance
Lightning Source LLC
Chambersburg PA
CBHW020051170426
43199CB00009B/246